The Belle's Stratagem by Hannah Cowley

A Comedy

As Acted At The Theatre-Royal in Covent-Garden.

Hannah Cowley was born Hannah Parkhouse on March 14th, 1743, the daughter of Hannah (née Richards) and Philip Parkhouse, a bookseller in Tiverton, Devon.

As one might expect details of much of her life are scant and that of her early life almost non-existent.

However, we do know that she married Thomas Cowley and that the couple moved to London where Thomas worked as an official in the Stamp Office and as a part-time journalist.

Her career in the literary world seemed to happen rather late. It was whilst the couple were attending a play, thought to be sometime in late 1775, that Cowley was struck by a sudden necessity to write.

Her first play, a comedy called The Runaway was sent to the famed actor-manager, David Garrick. It was produced at his final season at the Drury Lane theatre on February 15th, 1776. It was a success. She wrote her next two plays, the farce, Who's the Dupe? and the tragedy, Albina, before the year was out.

Getting these two plays into production took much longer and involved a very public spat with her rival Hannah More over whether Cowley's works had been plagarised by More.

Cowley wrote her most popular comedy in 1780; The Belle's Stratagem. It was staged at Covent Garden.

Her next play, The World as It Goes; or, a Party at Montpelier (the title was later changed to Second Thoughts Are Best) was unsuccessful, but she continued to write and there followed another seven plays; Which is the Man?; A Bold Stroke for a Husband; More Ways Than One; A School for Greybeards, or, The Mourning Bride; The Fate of Sparta, or, The Rival Kings; A Day in Turkey, or, The Russian Slaves and The Town Before You.

In 1801 Cowley published perhaps her greatest poetical work. A six-book epic "The Siege of Acre: An Epic Poem".

That same year Cowley retired to Tiverton in Devon, where she spent her remaining years out of the public spotlight whilst she quietly revised her plays.

Hannah Cowley died of liver failure on March 11th, 1809.

Index of Contents

TO THE QUEEN
DRAMATIS PERSONÆ
THE BELLE'S STRATAGEM
ACT I

D1521249

SCENE I.—Lincoln's-Inn
SCENE II.—A Hall at Doricourt's
SCENE IV.—An Apartment at Mr. Hardy's
ACT II
SCENE I. Sir George Touchwood's
SCENE changes to an Auction Room.—Busts, Pictures, &c. &c
ACT III
SCENE I. Mr. Hardy's
SCENE II.—Courtall's
SCENE III.—The Street
SCENE IV.—Sir George Touchwood's
ACT IV
SCENE I.—A Masquerade
SCENE II>—Courtall's
ACT V
SCENE I.—Hardy's
SCENE II.—Doricourt's
SCENE III.—Sir George Touchwood's
SCENE IV.—Doricourt's
SCENE V.—Hardy's
EPILOGUE
Hannah Cowley – A Short Biography
Hannah Cowley – A Concise Bibliography
Scenarios of Some of Her Plays

TO THE QUEEN

MADAM,

In the following Comedy, my purpose was, to draw a FEMALE CHARACTER, which with the most lively Sensibility, fine Understanding, and elegant Accomplishments, should unite that beautiful Reserve and Delicacy which, whilst they veil those charms, render them still more interesting. In delineating such a Character, my heart naturally dedicated it to YOUR MAJESTY; and nothing remained, but permission to lay it at Your feet. Your Majesty's graciously allowing me this high Honour, is the point to which my hopes aspired, and a reward, of which without censure I may be proud.

MADAM,

With the warmest wishes for the continuance of your Majesty's felicity,

I am
YOUR MAJESTY's
Most devoted and most dutiful Servant,
H. Cowley.

MEN.

DORICOURT,	Mr. Lewis.
HARDY,	Mr. Quick.
SIR GEORGE TOUCHWOOD,	Mr. Wroughton.
FLUTTER,	Mr. Lee Lewes.
SAVILLE,	Mr. Aickin.
VILLERS,	Mr. Whitfield.
COURTALL,	Mr. Robson.
SILVERTONGUE,	Mr. W. Bates.
CROWQUILL,	Mr. Jones.
FIRST GENTLEMAN,	Mr. Thompson.
SECOND GENTLEMAN,	Mr. L'Estrange.
MOUNTEBANK,	Mr. Booth.
FRENCH SERVANT,	Mr. Wewitzer.
PORTER,	Mr. Fearon.
DICK,	Mr. Stevens.

WOMEN.

LETITIA HARDY,	Miss Younge.
MRS. RACKET,	Mrs. Mattocks.
LADY FRANCES TOUCHWOOD,	Mrs. Hartley.
MISS OGLE,	Mrs. Morton.
KITTY WILLIS,	Miss Stewart.
LADY,	Mrs. Poussin.

MASQUERADERS, TRADESMEN, SERVANTS, &c.

THE BELLE'S STRATAGEM

ACT I

SCENE I.—Lincoln's-Inn

Enter **SAVILLE**, followed by a **SERVANT**, at the top of the stage, looking round, as if at a loss.

SAVILLE
Lincoln's-Inn!—Well, but where to find him, now I am in Lincoln's-Inn?—Where did he say his Master was?

SERVANT
He only said in Lincoln's-Inn, Sir.

SAVILLE

That's pretty! And your wisdom never enquired at whose chambers?

SERVANT

Sir, you spoke to the servant yourself.

SAVILLE

If I was too impatient to ask questions, you ought to have taken directions, blockhead!

Enter **COURTALL** singing.

Ha, Courtall!—Bid him keep the horses in motion, and then enquire at all the chambers round.

[Exit **SERVANT**.

What the devil brings you to this part of the town?—Have any of the Long Robes, handsome wives, sisters or chambermaids?

COURTALL

Perhaps they have;—but I came on a different errand; and, had thy good fortune brought thee here half an hour sooner, I'd have given thee such a treat, ha! ha! ha!

SAVILLE

I'm sorry I miss'd it: what was it?

COURTALL

I was informed a few days since, that my cousins Fallow were come to town, and desired earnestly to see me at their lodgings in Warwick-Court, Holborn. Away drove I, painting them all the way as so many Hebes. They came from the farthest part of Northumberland, had never been in town, and in course were made up of rusticity, innocence, and beauty.

SAVILLE

Well!

COURTALL

After waiting thirty minutes, during which there was a violent bustle, in bounced five fallow damsels, four of them maypoles;—the fifth, Nature, by way of variety, had bent in the Æsop style.—But they all opened at once, like hounds on a fresh scent:—"Oh, cousin Courtall!—How do you do, cousin Courtall! Lord, cousin, I am glad you are come! We want you to go with us to the Park, and the Plays, and the Opera, and Almack's, and all the fine places!"—The devil, thought I, my dears, may attend you, for I am sure I won't.—However, I heroically stayed an hour with them, and discovered, the virgins were all come to town with the hopes of leaving it—Wives:—their heads full of Knight-Baronights, Fops, and adventures.

SAVILLE

Well, how did you get off?

COURTALL

Oh, pleaded a million engagements.—However, conscience twitched me; so I breakfasted with them this morning, and afterwards 'squired them to the gardens here, as the most private place in town; and then took a sorrowful leave, complaining of my hard, hard fortune, that obliged me to set off immediately for Dorsetshire, ha! ha! ha!

SAVILLE

I congratulate your escape!—Courtall at Almack's, with five aukward country cousins! ha! ha! ha!—Why, your existence, as a Man of Gallantry, could never have survived it.

COURTALL

Death, and fire! had they come to town, like the rustics of the last age, to see Paul's, the Lions, and the Wax-work—at their service;—but the cousins of our days come up Ladies—and, with the knowledge they glean from magazines and pocket-books, Fine Ladies; laugh at the bashfulness of their grandmothers, and boldly demand their entrées in the first circles.

SAVILLE

Where can this fellow be!—Come, give me some news—I have been at war with woodcocks and partridges these two months, and am a stranger to all that has passed out of their region.

COURTALL

Oh! enough for three Gazettes. The Ladies are going to petition for a bill, that, during the war, every man may be allowed Two Wives.

SAVILLE

'Tis impossible they should succeed, for the majority of both Houses know what it is to have one.

COURTALL

Gallantry was black-ball'd at the Coterie last Thursday, and Prudence and Chastity voted in.

SAVILLE

Ay, that may hold 'till the Camps break up.—But have ye no elopements? no divorces?

COURTALL

Divorces are absolutely out, and the Commons-Doctors starving; so they are publishing trials of Crim. Con. with all the separate evidences at large; which they find has always a wonderful effect on their trade, actions tumbling in upon them afterwards, like mackarel at Gravesend.

SAVILLE

What more?

COURTALL

Nothing—for weddings, deaths, and politics, I never talk of, but whilst my hair is dressing. But prithee, Saville, how came you in town, whilst all the qualified gentry are playing at pop-gun on Coxheath, and the country over-run with hares and foxes?

SAVILLE

I came to meet my friend Doricourt, who, you know, is lately arrived from Rome.

COURTALL

Arrived! Yes, faith, and has cut us all out!—His carriage, his liveries, his dress, himself, are the rage of the day! His first appearance set the whole Ton in a ferment, and his valet is besieged by levées of taylors, habit-makers, and other Ministers of Fashion, to gratify the impatience of their customers for becoming à la mode de Doricourt. Nay, the beautiful Lady Frolic, t'other night, with two sister Countesses, insisted upon his waistcoat for muffs; and their snowy arms now bear it in triumph about town, to the heart-rending affliction of all our Beaux Garçons.

SAVILLE

Indeed! Well, those little gallantries will soon be over; he's on the point of marriage.

COURTALL

Marriage! Doricourt on the point of marriage! 'Tis the happiest tidings you could have given, next to his being hanged—Who is the Bride elect?

SAVILLE

I never saw her; but 'tis Miss Hardy, the rich heiress—the match was made by the parents, and the courtship begun on their nurses knees; Master used to crow at Miss, and Miss used to chuckle at Master.

COURTALL

Oh! then by this time they care no more for each other, than I do for my country cousins.

SAVILLE

I don't know that; they have never met since thus high, and so, probably, have some regard for each other.

COURTALL

Never met! Odd!

SAVILLE

A whim of Mr. Hardy's; he thought his daughter's charms would make a more forcible impression, if her lover remained in ignorance of them 'till his return from the Continent.

Enter Saville's **SERVANT**.

SERVANT

Mr. Doricourt, Sir, has been at Counsellor Pleadwell's, and gone about five minutes.

[Exit **SERVANT**.

SERVANT

Five minutes! Zounds! I have been five minutes too late all my life-time!—Good morrow, Courtall; I must pursue him.

(Going.)

COURTALL

Promise to dine with me to-day; I have some honest fellows.

(Going off on the opposite side.)

SAVILLE

Can't promise; perhaps I may.—See there, there's a bevy of female Patagonians, coming down upon us.

COURTALL

By the Lord, then, it must be my strapping cousins.—I dare not look behind me—Run, man, run.

[Exit, on the same side.

SCENE II.—A Hall at Doricourt's

(A gentle knock at the door.)

Enter the **PORTER**.

PORTER

Tap! What sneaking devil art thou?

(Opens the door.)

Enter **CROWQUILL**.

So! I suppose you are one of Monsieur's customers too? He's above stairs, now, overhauling all his Honour's things to a parcel of 'em.

CROWQUILL

No, Sir; it is with you, if you please, that I want to speak.

PORTER

Me! Well, what do you want with me?

CROWQUILL

Sir, you must know that I am—I am the Gentleman who writes the Tête-à-têtes in the Magazines.

PORTER

Oh, oh!—What, you are the fellow that ties folks together, in your sixpenny cuts, that never meet any where else?

CROWQUILL

Oh, dear Sir, excuse me!—we always go on foundation; and if you can help me to a few anecdotes of your master, such as what Marchioness he lost money to, in Paris—who is his favourite Lady in town— or the name of the Girl he first made love to at College—or any incidents that happened to his

Grandmother, or Great aunts—a couple will do, by way of supporters—I'll weave a web of intrigues, losses, and gallantries, between them, that shall fill four pages, procure me a dozen dinners, and you, Sir, a bottle of wine for your trouble.

PORTER
Oh, oh! I heard the butler talk of you, when I lived at Lord Tinket's. But what the devil do you mean by a bottle of wine!—You gave him a crown for a retaining fee.

CROWQUILL
Oh, Sir, that was for a Lord's amours; a Commoner's are never but half. Why, I have had a Baronet's for five shillings, though he was a married man, and changed his mistress every six weeks.

PORTER
Don't tell me! What signifies a Baronet, or a bit of a Lord, who, may be, was never further than sun and fun round London? We have travelled, man! My master has been in Italy, and over the whole island of Spain; talked to the Queen of France, and danced with her at a masquerade. Ay, and such folks don't go to masquerades for nothing; but mum—not a word more—Unless you'll rank my master with a Lord, I'll not be guilty of blabbing his secrets, I assure you.

CROWQUILL
Well, Sir, perhaps you'll throw in a hint or two of other families, where you've lived, that may be worked up into something; and so, Sir, here is one, two, three, four, five shillings.

PORTER
Well, that's honest, (pocketing the money.) To tell you the truth, I don't know much of my master's concerns yet;—but here comes Monsieur and his gang: I'll pump them: they have trotted after him all round Europe, from the Canaries to the Isle of Wight.

Enter several foreign **SERVANTS** and two **TRADESMEN**.

(The **PORTER** takes one of them aside.)

TRADESMAN
Well then, you have shew'd us all?

FRENCHMAN
All, en vérité, Messieurs! you avez seen every ting. Serviteur, serviteur.

[Exeunt **TRADESMEN**.

Ah, here comes one autre curious Englishman, and dat's one autre guinea pour moi.

Enter **SAVILLE**.

Allons, Monsieur, dis way; I will shew you tings, such tings you never see, begar, in England!—velvets by Le Mosse, suits cut by Verdue, trimmings by Grossette, embroidery by Detanville—

SAVILLE

Puppy!—where is your Master?

PORTER
Zounds! you chattering frog-eating dunderhead, can't you see a Gentleman?—'Tis Mr. Saville.

FRENCHMAN.
Monsieur Saville! Je suis mort de peur.—Ten thousand pardons! Excusez mon erreur, and permit me you conduct to Monsieur Doricourt; he be too happy à vous voir.

[Exeunt **FRENCHMAN** and **SAVILLE**.

PORTER
Step below a bit;—we'll make it out some-how!—I suppose a slice of sirloin won't make the story go down the worse.

[Exeunt **PORTER** and **CROWQUILL**.

SCENE III.—An Apartment at Doricourt's.

Enter **DORICOURT**.

DORICOURT (speaking to a **SERVANT** behind)
I shall be too late for St. James's; bid him come immediately.

Enter **FRENCHMAN** and **SAVILLE**.

FRENCHMAN
Monsieur Saville.

[Exit **FRENCHMAN**.

DORICOURT
Most fortunate! My dear Saville, let the warmth of this embrace speak the pleasure of my heart.

SAVILLE
Well, this is some comfort, after the scurvy reception I met with in your hall.—I prepared my mind, as I came up stairs, for a bon jour, a grimace, and an adieu.

DORICOURT
Why so?

SAVILLE
Judging of the master from the rest of the family. What the devil is the meaning of that flock of foreigners below, with their parchment faces and snuffy whiskers? What! can't an Englishman stand behind your carriage, buckle your shoe, or brush your coat?

DORICOURT

Stale, my dear Saville, stale! Englishmen make the best Soldiers, Citizens, Artizans, and Philosophers in the world; but the very worst Footmen. I keep French fellows and Germans, as the Romans kept slaves; because their own countrymen had minds too enlarged and haughty to descend with a grace to the duties of such a station.

SAVILLE

A good excuse for a bad practice.

DORICOURT

On my honour, experience will convince you of its truth. A Frenchman neither hears, sees, nor breathes, but as his master directs; and his whole system of conduct is compris'd in one short word, Obedience! An Englishman reasons, forms opinions, cogitates, and disputes; he is the mere creature of your will: the other, a being, conscious of equal importance in the universal scale with yourself, and is therefore your judge, whilst he wears your livery, and decides on your actions with the freedom of a censor.

SAVILLE

And this in defence of a custom I have heard you execrate, together with all the adventitious manners imported by our Travell'd Gentry.

DORICOURT

Ay, but that was at eighteen; we are always very wise at eighteen. But consider this point: we go into Italy, where the sole business of the people is to study and improve the powers of Music: we yield to the fascination, and grow enthusiasts in the charming science: we travel over France, and see the whole kingdom composing ornaments, and inventing Fashions: we condescend to avail ourselves of their industry, and adopt their modes: we return to England, and find the nation intent on the most important objects; Polity, Commerce, War, with all the Liberal Arts, employ her sons; the latent sparks glow afresh within our bosoms; the sweet follies of the Continent imperceptibly slide away, whilst Senators, Statesmen, Patriots and Heroes, emerge from the virtû of Italy, and the frippery of France.

SAVILLE

I may as well give it up! You had always the art of placing your faults in the best light; and I can't help loving you, faults and all: so, to start a subject which must please you, When do you expect Miss Hardy?

DORICOURT

Oh, the hour of expectation is past. She is arrived, and I this morning had the honour of an interview at Pleadwell's. The writings were ready; and, in obedience to the will of Mr. Hardy, we met to sign and seal.

SAVILLE

Has the event answered? Did your heart leap, or sink, when you beheld your Mistress?

DORICOURT

Faith, neither one nor t'other; she's a fine girl, as far as mere flesh and blood goes.—But—

SAVILLE

But what?

DORICOURT
Why, she's only a fine girl; complexion, shape, and features; nothing more.

SAVILLE
Is not that enough?

DORICOURT
No! she should have spirit! fire! l'air enjoué! that something, that nothing, which every body feels, and which no body can describe, in the resistless charmers of Italy and France.

SAVILLE
Thanks to the parsimony of my father, that kept me from travel! I would not have lost my relish for true unaffected English beauty, to have been quarrell'd for by all the Belles of Versailles and Florence.

DORICOURT
Pho! thou hast no taste. English beauty! 'Tis insipidity; it wants the zest, it wants poignancy, Frank! Why, I have known a Frenchwoman, indebted to nature for no one thing but a pair of decent eyes, reckon in her suite as many Counts, Marquisses, and Petits Maîtres, as would satisfy three dozen of our first-rate toasts. I have known an Italian Marquizina make ten conquests in stepping from her carriage, and carry her slaves from one city to another, whose real intrinsic beauty would have yielded to half the little Grisettes that pace your Mall on a Sunday.

SAVILLE
And has Miss Hardy nothing of this?

DORICOURT
If she has, she was pleased to keep it to herself. I was in the room half an hour before I could catch the colour of her eyes; and every attempt to draw her into conversation occasioned so cruel an embarrassment, that I was reduced to the necessity of news, French fleets, and Spanish captures, with her father.

SAVILLE
So Miss Hardy, with only beauty, modesty, and merit, is doom'd to the arms of a husband who will despise her.

DORICOURT
You are unjust. Though she has not inspir'd me with violent passion, my honour secures her felicity.

SAVILLE
Come, come, Doricourt, you know very well that when the honour of a husband is locum-tenens for his heart, his wife must be as indifferent as himself, if she is not unhappy.

DORICOURT
Pho! never moralise without spectacles. But, as we are upon the tender subject, how did you bear Touchwood's carrying Lady Frances?

SAVILLE
You know I never look'd up to her with hope, and Sir George is every way worthy of her.

DORICOURT

A la mode Angloise, a philosopher even in love.

SAVILLE

Come, I detain you—you seem dress'd at all points, and of course have an engagement.

DORICOURT

To St. James's. I dine at Hardy's, and accompany them to the masquerade in the evening: but breakfast with me to-morrow, and we'll talk of our old companions; for I swear to you, Saville, the air of the Continent has not effaced one youthful prejudice or attachment.

SAVILLE

With an exception to the case of Ladies and Servants.

DORICOURT

True; there I plead guilty:—but I have never yet found any man whom I could cordially take to my heart, and call Friend, who was not born beneath a British sky, and whose heart and manners were not truly English.

[Exit **DORICOURT** and **SAVILLE**.

SCENE IV.—An Apartment at Mr. Hardy's

VILLIERS seated on a sopha, reading.

Enter **FLUTTER**.

FLUTTER

Hah, Villers, have you seen Mrs. Racket?—Miss Hardy, I find, is out.

VILLERS

I have not seen her yet. I have made a voyage to Lapland since I came in. (flinging away the book.) A Lady at her toilette is as difficult to be moved, as a Quaker, (yawning). What events have happened in the world since yesterday? have you heard?

FLUTTER

Oh, yes; I stopt at Tattersall's as I came by, and there I found Lord James Jessamy, Sir William Wilding, and Mr.—. But, now I think of it, you sha'n't know a syllable of the matter; for I have been informed you never believe above one half of what I say.

VILLERS

My dear fellow, somebody has imposed upon you most egregiously!—Half! Why, I never believe one tenth part of what you say; that is, according to the plain and literal expression: but, as I understand you, your intelligence is amusing.

FLUTTER

That's very hard now, very hard. I never related a falsity in my life, unless I stumbled on it by mistake; and if it were otherwise, your dull matter-of-fact people are infinitely oblig'd to those warm imaginations which soar into fiction to amuse you; for, positively, the common events of this little dirty world are not worth talking about, unless you embellish 'em!—Hah! here comes Mrs. Racket: Adieu to weeds, I see! All life!

Enter **MRS RACKET**.

Enter, Madam, in all your charms! Villers has been abusing your toilette for keeping you so long; but I think we are much oblig'd to it, and so are you.

MRS RACKET

How so, pray? Good-morning t'ye both. Here, here's a hand a-piece for you.

(They kiss her hands.)

FLUTTER

How so! Because it has given you so many beauties.

MRS RACKET

Delightful compliment! What do you think of that, Villers?

VILLERS

That he and his compliments are alike—shewy, but won't bear examining.—So you brought Miss Hardy to town last night?

MRS RACKET

Yes, I should have brought her before, but I had a fall from my horse, that confined me a week.—I suppose in her heart she wished me hanged a dozen times an hour.

FLUTTER

Why?

MRS RACKET

Had she not an expecting Lover in town all the time? She meets him this morning at the Lawyer's.—I hope she'll charm him; she's the sweetest girl in the world.

VILLERS

Vanity, like murder, will out.—You have convinced me you think yourself more charming.

MRS RACKET

How can that be?

VILLERS

No woman ever praises another, unless she thinks herself superior in the very perfections she allows.

FLUTTER

Nor no man ever rails at the sex, unless he is conscious he deserves their hatred.

MRS RACKET
Thank ye, Flutter—I'll owe ye a bouquet for that. I am going to visit the new-married Lady Frances Touchwood.—Who knows her husband?

FLUTTER
Every body.

MRS RACKET
Is there not something odd in his character?

VILLERS
Nothing, but that he is passionately fond of his wife;—and so petulant is his love, that he open'd the cage of a favourite Bullfinch, and sent it to catch Butterflies, because she rewarded its song with her kisses.

MRS RACKET
Intolerable monster! Such a brute deserves—

VILLERS
Nay, nay, nay, nay, this is your sex now—Give a woman but one stroke of character, off she goes, like a ball from a racket; sees the whole man, marks him down for an angel or a devil, and so exhibits him to her acquaintance.—This monster! this brute! is one of the worthiest fellows upon earth; sound sense, and a liberal mind; but doats on his wife to such excess, that he quarrels with every thing she admires, and is jealous of her tippet and nosegay.

MRS RACKET
Oh, less love for me, kind Cupid! I can see no difference between the torment of such an affection, and hatred.

FLUTTER
Oh, pardon me, inconceivable difference, inconceivable; I see it as clearly as your bracelet. In the one case the husband would say, as Mr. Snapper said t'other day, Zounds! Madam, do you suppose that my table, and my house, and my pictures!—A-propos, des Bottes. There was the divinest Plague of Athens sold yesterday at Langford's! the dead figures so natural, you would have sworn they had been alive! Lord Primrose bid Five hundred—Six, said Lady Carmine.—A thousand, said Ingot the Nabob.—Down went the hammer.—A rouleau for your bargain, said Sir Jeremy Jingle. And what answer do you think Ingot made him?

MRS RACKET
Why, took the offer.

FLUTTER
Sir, I would oblige you, but I buy this picture to place in the nursery: the children have already got Whittington and his Cat; 'tis just this size, and they'll make good companions.

MRS RACKET

Ha! ha! ha! Well, I protest that's just the way now—the Nabobs and their wives outbid one at every sale, and the creatures have no more taste—

VILLERS

There again! You forget this story is told by Flutter, who always remembers every thing but the circumstances and the person he talks about:—'twas Ingot who offer'd a rouleau for the bargain, and Sir Jeremy Jingle who made the reply.

FLUTTER

Egad, I believe you are right.—Well, the story is as good one way as t'other, you know. Good morning. I am going to Mrs. Crotchet's concert, and in my way back shall make my bow at Sir George's.

(Going.)

VILLERS

I'll venture every figure in your taylor's bill, you make some blunder there.

FLUTTER (turning back)

Done! My taylor's bill has not been paid these two years; and I'll open my mouth with as much care as Mrs. Bridget Button, who wears cork plumpers in each cheek, and never hazards more than six words for fear of shewing them.

[Exit **FLUTTER**.

MRS RACKET

'Tis a good-natur'd insignificant creature! let in every where, and cared for no where.—There's Miss Hardy return'd from Lincoln's-Inn:—she seems rather chagrin'd.

VILLERS

Then I leave you to your communications.

Enter **LETITIA**, followed by her **MAID**.

Adieu! I am rejoiced to see you so well, Madam! but I must tear myself away.

LETITIA

Don't vanish in a moment.

VILLERS

Oh, inhuman! you are two of the most dangerous women in town.—Staying here to be cannonaded by four such eyes, is equal to a rencontre with Paul Jones, or a midnight march to Omoa!—They'll swallow the nonsense for the sake of the compliment. (Aside.)

[Exit **VILLERS**.

LETITIA (gives her cloak to her maid.)

Order Du Quesne never to come again; he shall positively dress my hair no more.

[Exit Maid.]

And this odious silk, how unbecoming it is!—I was bewitched to chuse it.

(Throwing herself on a sopha, and looking in a pocket-glass, MRS RACKET staring at her.)

Did you ever see such a fright as I am to-day?

MRS RACKET
Yes, I have seen you look much worse.

LETITIA
How can you be so provoking? If I do not look this morning worse than ever I look'd in my life, I am naturally a fright. You shall have it which way you will.

MRS RACKET
Just as you please; but pray what is the meaning of all this?

LETITIA (rising.)
Men are all dissemblers! flatterers! deceivers! Have I not heard a thousand times of my air, my eyes, my shape—all made for victory! and to-day, when I bent my whole heart on one poor conquest, I have proved that all those imputed charms amount to nothing;—for Doricourt saw them unmov'd.—A husband of fifteen months could not have examined me with more cutting indifference.

MRS RACKET
Then you return it like a wife of fifteen months, and be as indifferent as he.

LETITIA
Aye, there's the sting! The blooming boy, who left his image in my young heart, is at four and twenty improv'd in every grace that fix'd him there. It is the same face that my memory, and my dreams, constantly painted to me; but its graces are finished, and every beauty heightened. How mortifying, to feel myself at the same moment his slave, and an object of perfect indifference to him!

MRS RACKET
How are you certain that was the case? Did you expect him to kneel down before the lawyer, his clerks, and, your father, to make oath of your beauty?

LETITIA
No; but he should have look'd as if a sudden ray had pierced him! he should have been breathless! speechless! for, oh! Caroline, all this was I.

MRS RACKET
I am sorry you was such a fool. Can you expect a man, who has courted and been courted by half the fine women in Europe, to feel like a girl from a boarding-school? He is the prettiest fellow you have seen, and in course bewilders your imagination; but he has seen a million of pretty women, child, before he saw you; and his first feelings have been over long ago.

LETITIA
Your raillery distresses me; but I will touch his heart, or never be his wife.

MRS RACKET
Absurd, and romantic! If you have no reason to believe his heart pre-engaged, be satisfied; if he is a man of honour, you'll have nothing to complain of.

LETITIA
Nothing to complain of! Heav'ns! shall I marry the man I adore, with such an expectation as that?

MRS RACKET
And when you have fretted yourself pale, my dear, you'll
have mended your expectation greatly.

LETITIA (pausing.)
Yet I have one hope. If there is any power whose peculiar care is faithful love, that power I invoke to aid me.

Enter **MR HARDY**.

MR HARDY
Well, now; wasn't I right? Aye, Letty! Aye, Cousin Racket! wasn't I right? I knew 'twould be so. He was all agog to see her before he went abroad; and, if he had, he'd have thought no more of her face, may be, than his own.

MRS RACKET
May be, not half so much.

MR HARDY
Aye, may be so:—but I see into things; exactly as I foresaw, to-day he fell desperately in love with the wench, he! he! he!

LETITIA
Indeed, Sir! how did you perceive it?

MR HARDY
That's a pretty question! How do I perceive every thing? How did I foresee the fall of corn, and the rise of taxes? How did I know, that if we quarrelled with America, Norway deals would be dearer? How did I foretell that a war would sink the funds? How did I forewarn Parson Homily, that if he didn't some way or other contrive to get more votes than Rubrick, he'd lose the lectureship? How did I—But what the devil makes you so dull, Letitia? I thought to have found you popping about as brisk as the jacks of your harpsichord.

LETITIA
Surely, Sir, 'tis a very serious occasion.

MR HARDY
Pho, pho! girls should never be grave before marriage. How did you feel, Cousin, beforehand? Aye!

MRS RACKET

Feel! why exceedingly full of cares.

MR HARDY

Did you?

MRS RACKET

I could not sleep for thinking of my coach, my liveries, and my chairmen; the taste of clothes I should be presented in, distracted me for a week; and whether I should be married in white or lilac, gave me the most cruel anxiety.

LETITIA

And is it possible that you felt no other care?

MR HARDY

And pray, of what sort may your cares be, Mrs. Letitia? I begin to foresee now that you have taken a dislike to Doricourt.

LETITIA

Indeed, Sir, I have not.

MR HARDY

Then what's all this melancholy about? A'n't you going to be married? and, what's more, to a sensible man? and, what's more to a young girl, to a handsome man? And what's all this melancholy for, I say?

MRS RACKET

Why, because he is handsome and sensible, and because she's over head and ears in love with him; all which, it seems, your foreknowledge had not told you a word of.

LETITIA

Fye, Caroline!

MR HARDY

Well, come, do you tell me what's the matter then? If you don't like him, hang the signing and sealing, he sha'n't have ye:—and yet I can't say that neither; for you know that estate, that cost his father and me upwards of fourscore thousand pounds, must go all to him if you won't have him: if he won't have you, indeed, 'twill be all yours. All that's clear, engross'd upon parchment, and the poor dear man set his hand to it whilst he was a dying.—"Ah!" said I, "I foresee you'll never live to see 'em come together; but their first son shall be christened Jeremiah after you, that I promise you."—But come, I say, what is the matter? Don't you like him?

LETITIA

I fear, Sir—if I must speak—I fear I was less agreeable in Mr. Doricourt's eyes, than he appeared in mine.

MR HARDY

There you are mistaken; for I asked him, and he told me he liked you vastly. Don't you think he must have taken a fancy to her?

MRS RACKET

Why really I think so, as I was not by.

LETITIA

My dear Sir, I am convinced he has not; but if there is spirit or invention in woman, he shall.

MR HARDY

Right, Girl; go to your toilette—

LETITIA

It is not my toilette that can serve me: but a plan has struck me, if you will not oppose it, which flatters me with brilliant success.

MR HARDY

Oppose it! not I indeed! What is it?

LETITIA

Why, Sir—it may seem a little paradoxical; but, as he does not like me enough, I want him to like me still less, and will at our next interview endeavour to heighten his indifference into dislike.

MR HARDY

Who the devil could have foreseen that?

MRS RACKET

Heaven and earth! Letitia, are you serious?

LETITIA

As serious as the most important business of my life demands.

MRS RACKET

Why endeavour to make him dislike you?

LETITIA

Because 'tis much easier to convert a sentiment into its opposite, than to transform indifference into tender passion.

MRS RACKET

That may be good philosophy, but I am afraid you'll find it a bad maxim.

LETITIA

I have the strongest confidence in it. I am inspired with unusual spirits, and on this hazard willingly stake my chance for happiness. I am impatient to begin my measures. [Exit Letitia.

MR HARDY

Can you foresee the end of this, Cousin?

MRS RACKET

No, Sir; nothing less than your penetration can do that, I am sure; and I can't stay now to consider it. I am going to call on the Ogles, and then to Lady Frances Touchwood's, and then to an Auction, and then—I don't know where—but I shall be at home time enough to witness this extraordinary interview. Good-bye.

[Exit **MRS RACKET**.

MR HARDY
Well, 'tis an odd thing—I can't understand it—but I foresee Letty will have her way, and so I sha'n't give myself the trouble to dispute it.

[Exit **MR HARDY**.

ACT II

SCENE I. Sir George Touchwood's

Enter **DORICOURT** and **SIR GEORGE**.

DORICOURT
Married, ha! ha! ha! you, whom I heard in Paris say such things of the sex, are in London a married man.

SIR GEORGE
The sex is still what it has ever been since la petite morale banished substantial virtues; and rather than have given my name to one of your high-bred fashionable dames, I'd have crossed the line in a fire-ship, and married a Japanese.

DORICOURT
Yet you have married an English beauty, yea, and a beauty born in high life.

SIR GEORGE
True; but she has a simplicity of heart and manners, that would have become the fair Hebrew damsels toasted by the Patriarchs.

DORICOURT
Ha! ha! Why, thou art a downright matrimonial Quixote. My life on't, she becomes as mere a Town Lady in six months as though she had been bred to the trade.

SIR GEORGE
Common—common—(contemptuously). No, Sir, Lady Frances despises high life so much from the ideas I have given her, that she'll live in it like a salamander in fire.

DORICOURT
Oh, that the circle dans la place Victoire could witness thy extravagance! I'll send thee off to St. Evreux this night, drawn at full length, and coloured after nature.

SIR GEORGE

Tell him then, to add to the ridicule, that Touchwood glories in the name of Husband; that he has found in one Englishwoman more beauty than Frenchmen ever saw, and more goodness than Frenchwomen can conceive.

DORICOURT

Well—enough of description. Introduce me to this phœnix; I came on purpose.

SIR GEORGE

Introduce!—oh, aye, to be sure—I believe Lady Frances is engaged just now—but another time. How handsome the dog looks to-day! Aside.

DORICOURT

Another time!—but I have no other time. 'Sdeath! this is the only hour I can command this fortnight!

SIR GEORGE

[Aside.] I am glad to hear it, with all my soul. So then, you can't dine with us to-day? That's very unlucky.

DORICOURT

Oh, yes—as to dinner—yes, I can, I believe, contrive to dine with you to-day.

SIR GEORGE

Psha! I didn't think on what I was saying; I meant supper.—You can't sup with us?

DORICOURT

Why, supper will be rather more convenient than dinner.—But you are fortunate—if you had ask'd me any other night, I could not have come.

SIR GEORGE

To-night!—Gad, now I recollect, we are particularly engaged to-night.—But to-morrow night—

DORICOURT

Why look ye, Sir George, 'tis very plain you have no inclination to let me see your wife at all; so here I sit (throws himself on a sopha.)—There's my hat, and here are my legs.—Now I sha'n't stir till I have seen her; and I have no engagements: I'll breakfast, dine, and sup with you every day this week.

SIR GEORGE

Was there ever such a provoking wretch! But, to be plain with you, Doricourt, I and my house are at your service: but you are a damn'd agreeable fellow, and ten years younger than I am; and the women, I observe, always simper when you appear. For these reasons, I had rather, when Lady Frances and I are together, that you should forget we are acquainted, further than a nod, a smile, or a how-d'ye.

DORICOURT

Very well.

SIR GEORGE

It is not merely yourself in propriâ personâ that I object to; but, if you are intimate here, you'll make my house still more the fashion than it is; and it is already so much so, that my doors are of no use to me. I married Lady Frances to engross her to myself; yet such is the blessed freedom of modern manners, that, in spite of me, her eyes, thoughts, and conversation, are continually divided amongst all the Flirts and Coxcombs of Fashion.

DORICOURT
To be sure, I confess that kind of freedom is carried rather too far. 'Tis hard one can't have a jewel in one's cabinet, but the whole town must be gratified with its lustre. He sha'n't preach me out of seeing his wife, though. [Aside.

SIR GEORGE
Well, now, that's reasonable. When you take time to reflect, Doricourt, I always observe you decide right, and therefore I hope—

Enter **SERVANT**.

SERVANT
Sir, my Lady desires—

SIR GEORGE
I am particularly engaged.

DORICOURT
Oh, Lord, that shall be no excuse in the world (leaping from the sopha). Lead the way, John.—I'll attend your Lady.

[Exit, following the **SERVANT**.

SIR GEORGE
What devil possessed me to talk about her!—Here, Doricourt!

(Running after him.)

Doricourt!

Enter **MRS RACKET**, and **MISS OGLE**, followed by a **SERVANT**.

MRS RACKET
Acquaint your Lady, that Mrs. Racket, and Miss Ogle, are here.

[Exit **SERVANT**.

MISS OGLE
I shall hardly know Lady Frances, 'tis so long since I was in Shropshire.

MRS RACKET
And I'll be sworn you never saw her out of Shropshire.—Her father kept her locked up with his Caterpillars and Shells; and loved her beyond any thing—but a blue Butterfly, and a petrified Frog!

MISS OGLE
Ha! ha! ha!—Well, 'twas a cheap way of breeding her:—you know he was very poor, though a Lord; and very high-spirited, though a Virtuoso.—In town, her Pantheons, Operas, and Robes de Cour, would have swallowed his Sea-Weeds, Moths, and Monsters, in six weeks!—Sir George, I find, thinks his Wife a most extraordinary creature: he has taught her to despise every thing like Fashionable Life, and boasts that example will have no effect on her.

MRS RACKET
There's a great degree of impertinence in all that—I'll try to make her a Fine Lady, to humble him.

MISS OGLE
That's just the thing I wish.

Enter **LADY FRANCES**.

LADY FRANCES
I beg ten thousand pardons, my dear Mrs. Racket.—Miss Ogle, I rejoice to see you: I should have come to you sooner, but I was detained in conversation by Mr. Doricourt.

MRS RACKET
Pray make no apology; I am quite happy that we have your Ladyship in town at last.—What stay do you make?

LADY FRANCES
A short one! Sir George talks with regret of the scenes we have left; and as the ceremony of presentation is over, will, I believe, soon return.

MISS OGLE
Sure he can't be so cruel! Does your Ladyship wish to return so soon?

LADY FRANCES
I have not the habit of consulting my own wishes; but, I think, if they decide, we shall not return immediately. I have yet hardly form'd an idea of London.

MRS RACKET
I shall quarrel with your Lord and Master, if he dares think of depriving us of you so soon. How do you dispose of yourself to-day?

LADY FRANCES
Sir George is going with me this morning to the mercer's, to chuse a silk; and then—

MRS RACKET
Chuse a silk for you! ha! ha! ha! Sir George chuses your laces too, I hope; your gloves, and your pincushions!

LADY FRANCES
Madam!

MRS RACKET

I am glad to see you blush, my dear Lady Frances. These are strange homespun ways! If you do these things, pray keep 'em secret. Lord bless us! If the Town should know your husband chuses your gowns!

MISS OGLE

You are very young, my Lady, and have been brought up in solitude. The maxims you learnt among the Wood-Nymphs in Shropshire, won't pass current here, I assure you.

MRS RACKET

Why, my dear creature, you look quite frighten'd!—Come, you shall go with us to an Exhibition, and an Auction.—Afterwards, we'll take a turn in the Park, and then drive to Kensington;—so we shall be at home by four, to dress; and in the evening I'll attend you to Lady Brilliant's masquerade.

LADY FRANCES

I shall be very happy to be of your party, if Sir George has no engagements.

MRS RACKET

What! Do you stand so low in your own opinion, that you dare not trust yourself without Sir George! If you chuse to play Darby and Joan, my dear, you should have stay'd in the country;—'tis an Exhibition not calculated for London, I assure you!

MISS OGLE

What I suppose, my Lady, you and Sir George, will be seen pacing it comfortably round the Canal, arm and arm, and then go lovingly into the same carriage;—dine tête-à-tête, spend the evening at Picquet, and so go soberly to bed at Eleven!—Such a snug plan may do for an Attorney and his Wife; but, for Lady Frances Touchwood, 'tis as unsuitable as linsey-woolsey, or a black bonnet at the Festino!

LADY FRANCES

These are rather new doctrines to me!—But, my dear Mrs. Racket, you and Miss Ogle must judge of these things better than I can. As you observe, I am but young, and may have caught absurd opinions.—Here is Sir George!

Enter **SIR GEORGE**.

SIR GEORGE (Aside.)
'Sdeath! another room full!

LADY FRANCES

My love! Mrs. Racket, and Miss Ogle.

MRS RACKET

Give you joy, Sir George.—We came to rob you of Lady Frances for a few hours.

SIR GEORGE

A few hours!

LADY FRANCES

Oh, yes! I am going to an Exhibition, and an Auction, and the Park, and Kensington, and a thousand places!—It is quite ridiculous, I find, for married people to be always together—We shall be laughed at!

SIR GEORGE
I am astonished!—Mrs. Racket, what does the dear creature mean?

MRS RACKET
Mean, Sir George!—what she says, I imagine.

MISS OGLE
Why, you know, Sir, as Lady Frances had the misfortune to be bred entirely in the Country, she cannot be supposed to be versed in Fashionable Life.

SIR GEORGE
No; heaven forbid she should!—If she had, Madam, she would never have been my Wife!

MRS RACKET
Are you serious?

SIR GEORGE
Perfectly so.—I should never have had the courage to have married a well-bred Fine Lady.

MISS OGLE
Pray, Sir, what do you take a Fine Lady to be, that you express such fear of her? (sneeringly.)

SIR GEORGE
A being easily described, Madam, as she is seen every where, but in her own house. She sleeps at home, but she lives all over the town. In her mind, every sentiment gives place to the Lust of Conquest, and the vanity of being particular. The feelings of Wife, and Mother, are lost in the whirl of dissipation. If she continues virtuous, 'tis by chance—and if she preserves her Husband from ruin, 'tis by her dexterity at the Card-Table!—Such a Woman I take to be a perfect Fine Lady!

MRS RACKET
And you I take to be a slanderous Cynic of two-and-thirty.—Twenty years hence, one might have forgiven such a libel!—Now, Sir, hear my definition of a Fine Lady:—She is a creature for whom Nature has done much, and Education more; she has Taste, Elegance, Spirit, Understanding. In her manner she is free, in her morals nice. Her behaviour is undistinguishingly polite to her Husband, and all mankind;—her sentiments are for their hours of retirement. In a word, a Fine Lady is the life of conversation, the spirit of society, the joy of the public!—Pleasure follows where ever she appears, and the kindest wishes attend her slumbers.—Make haste, then, my dear Lady Frances, commence Fine Lady, and force your Husband to acknowledge the justness of my picture!

LADY FRANCES
I am sure 'tis a delightful one. How can you dislike it, Sir George? You painted Fashionable Life in colours so disgusting, that I thought I hated it; but, on a nearer view, it seems charming. I have hitherto lived in obscurity; 'tis time that I should be a Woman of the World. I long to begin;—my heart pants with expectation and delight!

MRS RACKET
Come, then; let us begin directly. I am inpatient to introduce you to that Society, which you were born to ornament and charm.

LADY FRANCES
Adieu! my Love!—We shall meet again at dinner.

(Going.)

SIR GEORGE
Sure, I am in a dream!—Fanny!

LADY FRANCES (returning)
Sir George?

SIR GEORGE
Will you go without me?

MRS RACKET
Will you go without me!—ha! ha! ha! what a pathetic address! Why, sure you would not always be seen side by side, like two beans upon a stalk. Are you afraid to trust Lady Frances with me, Sir?

SIR GEORGE
Heaven and earth! with whom can a man trust his wife, in the present state of society? Formerly there were distinctions of character amongst ye: every class of females had its particular description; Grandmothers were pious, Aunts, discreet, Old Maids censorious! but now aunts, grandmothers, girls, and maiden gentlewomen, are all the same creature;—a wrinkle more or less is the sole difference between ye.

MRS RACKET
That Maiden Gentlewomen have lost their censoriousness, is surely not in your catalogue of grievances.

SIR GEORGE
Indeed it is—and ranked amongst the most serious grievances.—Things went well, Madam, when the tongues of three or four old Virgins kept all the Wives and Daughters of a parish in awe. They were the Dragons that guarded the Hesperian fruit; and I wonder they have not been oblig'd, by act of parliament, to resume their function.

MRS RACKET
Ha! ha! ha! and pension'd, I suppose, for making strict enquiries into the lives and conversations of their neighbours.

SIR GEORGE
With all my heart, and impowered to oblige every woman to conform her conduct to her real situation. You, for instance, are a Widow: your air should be sedate, your dress grave, your deportment matronly, and in all things an example to the young women growing up about you!—instead of which, you are dress'd for conquest, think of nothing but ensnaring hearts; are a Coquette, a Wit, and a Fine Lady.

MRS RACKET

Bear witness to what he says! A Coquette! a Wit! and a Fine Lady! Who would have expected an eulogy from such an ill-natur'd mortal!—Valour to a Soldier, Wisdom to a Judge, or glory to a Prince, is not more than such a character to a Woman.

MISS OGLE

Sir George, I see, languishes for the charming society of a century and a half ago; when a grave 'Squire, and a still graver Dame, surrounded by a sober family, form'd a stiff groupe in a mouldy old house in the corner of a Park.

MRS RACKET

Delightful serenity! Undisturb'd by any noise but the cawing of rooks, and the quarterly rumbling of an old family-coach on a state-visit; with the happy intervention of a friendly call from the Parish Apothecary, or the Curate's Wife.

SIR GEORGE

And what is the society of which you boast?—a meer chaos, in which all distinction of rank is lost in a ridiculous affectation of ease, and every different order of beings huddled together, as they were before the creation. In the same select party, you will often find the wife of a Bishop and a Sharper, of an Earl and a Fidler. In short, 'tis one universal masquerade, all disguised in the same habits and manners.

SERVANT

Mr. Flutter.

[Exit **SERVANT**.

SIR GEORGE

Here comes an illustration. Now I defy you to tell from his appearance, whether Flutter is a Privy Counsellor or a Mercer, a Lawyer, or a Grocer's 'Prentice.

Enter **FLUTTER**.

FLUTTER

Oh, just which you please, Sir George; so you don't make me a Lord Mayor. Ah, Mrs. Racket!—Lady Frances, your most obedient; you look—now hang me, if that's not provoking!—had your gown been of another colour, I would have said the prettiest thing you ever heard in your life.

MISS OGLE

Pray give it us.

FLUTTER

I was yesterday at Mrs. Bloomer's. She was dress'd all in green; no other colour to be seen but that of her face and bosom. So says I, My dear Mrs. Bloomer! you look like a Carnation, just bursting from its pod.

SIR GEORGE

And what said her Husband?

FLUTTER
Her Husband! Why, her Husband laugh'd, and said a Cucumber would have been a happier simile.

SIR GEORGE
But there are Husbands, Sir, who would rather have corrected than amended your comparison; I, for instance, should consider a man's complimenting my Wife as an impertinence.

FLUTTER
Why, what harm can there be in compliments? Sure they are not infectious; and, if they were, you, Sir George, of all people breathing, have reason to be satisfied about your Lady's attachment; every body talks of it: that little Bird there, that she killed out of jealousy, the most extraordinary instance of affection, that ever was given.

LADY FRANCES
I kill a Bird through jealousy!—Heavens! Mr. Flutter, how can you impute such a cruelty to me?

SIR GEORGE
I could have forgiven you, if you had.

FLUTTER
Oh, what a blundering Fool!—No, no—now I remember—'twas your Bird, Lady Frances—that's it; your Bullfinch, which Sir George, in one of the refinements of his passion, sent into the wide world to seek its fortune.—He took it for a Knight in disguise.

LADY FRANCES
Is it possible! O, Sir George, could I have imagin'd it was you who depriv'd me of a creature I was so fond of?

SIR GEORGE
Mr. Flutter, you are one of those busy, idle, meddling people, who, from mere vacuity of mind, are, the most dangerous inmates in a family. You have neither feelings nor opinions of your own; but, like a glass in a tavern, bear about those of every Blockhead, who gives you his;—and, because you mean no harm, think yourselves excus'd, though broken friendships, discords, and murders, are the consequences of your indiscretions.

FLUTTER (taking out his Tablets)
Vacuity of Mind!—What was the next? I'll write down this sermon; 'tis the first I have heard since my Grandmother's funeral.

MISS OGLE
Come, Lady Frances, you see what a cruel creature your loving Husband can be; so let us leave him.

SIR GEORGE
Madam, Lady Frances shall not go.

LADY FRANCES
Shall not, Sir George?—This is the first time such an expression—(weeping)

SIR GEORGE
My love! my life!

LADY FRANCES
Don't imagine I'll be treated like a Child! denied what I wish, and then pacified with sweet words.

MISS OGLE (apart)
The Bullfinch! that's an excellent subject; never let it down.

LADY FRANCES
I see plainly you would deprive me of every pleasure, as well as of my sweet Bird—out of pure love!—Barbarous Man!

SIR GEORGE
'Tis well, Madam;—your resentment of that circumstance proves to me, what I did not before suspect, that you are deficient both in tenderness and understanding.—Tremble to think the hour approaches, in which you would give worlds for such a proof of my love. Go, Madam, give yourself to the Public; abandon your heart to dissipation, and see if, in the scenes of gaiety and folly that await you, you can find a recompence for the lost affection of a doating Husband.

[Exit **SIR GEORGE**.

FLUTTER
Lord! what a fine thing it is to have the gift of Speech! I suppose Sir George practises at Coachmakers-hall, or the Black-horse in Bond-street.

LADY FRANCES
He is really angry; I cannot go.

MRS RACKET
Not go! Foolish Creature! you are arrived at the moment, which some time or other was sure to happen; and everything depends on the use you make of it.

MISS OGLE
Come, Lady Frances! don't hesitate!—the minutes are precious.

LADY FRANCES
I could find in my heart!—and yet I won't give up neither.—If I should in this instance, he'll expect it for ever.

[Exeunt **LADY FRANCES**, and **MRS RACKET**.

MISS OGLE
Now you act like a Woman of Spirit.

[Exeunt **MISS OGLE**, and **MRS RACKET**.

FLUTTER

A fair tug, by Jupiter—between Duty and Pleasure!—Pleasure beats, and off we go, Iö triumphe!

[Exit **FLUTTER**.

SCENE changes to an Auction Room.—Busts, Pictures, &c. &c

Enter **SILVERTONGUE** with three **PUFFERS**.

SILVERTONGUE
Very well,—very well.—This morning will be devoted to curiosity; my sale begins to-morrow at eleven. But, Mrs. Fagg, if you do no better than you did in Lord Fillagree's sale, I shall discharge you.—You want a knack terribly: and this dress—why, nobody can mistake you for a Gentlewoman.

MRS FAGG
Very true, Mr. Silvertongue; but I can't dress like a Lady upon Half-a-crown a day, as the saying is.—If you want me to dress like a Lady, you must double my pay.—Double or quits, Mr. Silvertongue.

SILVERTONGUE
—Five Shillings a day! what a demand! Why, Woman, there are a thousand Parsons in the town, who don't make Five Shillings a day; though they preach, pray, christen, marry, and bury, for the Good of the Community.—Five Shillings a day!—why, 'tis the pay of a Lieutenant in a marching Regiment, who keeps a Servant, a Mistress, a Horse; fights, dresses, ogles, makes love, and dies upon Five Shillings a day.

MRS FAGG
Oh, as to that, all that's very right. A Soldier should not be too fond of life; and forcing him to do all these things upon Five Shillings a day, is the readiest way to make him tir'd on't.

SILVERTONGUE
Well, Mask, have you been looking into the Antiquaries?—have you got all the terms of art in a string—aye?

MASK
Yes, I have: I know the Age of a Coin by the taste; and can fix the Birth-day of a Medal, Anno Mundi or Anno Domini, though the green rust should have eaten up every character. But you know, the brown suit and the wig I wear when I personate the Antiquary, are in Limbo.

SILVERTONGUE
Those you have on, may do.

MASK
These!—Why, in these I am a young travell'd Cognoscento: Mr. Glib bought them of Sir Tom Totter's Valet; and I am going there directly. You know his Picture-Sale comes on to-day; and I have got my head full of Parmegiano, Sal Rosa, Metzu, Tarbaek, and Vandermeer. I talk of the relief of Woovermans, the spirit of Teniers, the colouring of the Venetian School, and the correctness of the Roman. I distinguish Claude by his Sleep, and Ruysdael by his Water. The rapidity of Tintoret's pencil strikes me at the first glance; whilst the harmony of Vandyk, and the glow of Correggio, point out their Masters.

Enter **COMPANY**.

1st LADY
Hey-day, Mr. Silvertongue! what, nobody here!

SILVERTONGUE
Oh, my Lady, we shall have company enough in a trice; if your carriage is seen at my door, no other will pass it, I am sure.

1st LADY
Familiar Monster! [Aside.] That's a beautiful Diana, Mr. Silvertongue; but in the name of Wonder, how came Actæon to be placed on the top of a House?

SILVERTONGUE
That's a David and Bathsheba, Ma'am.

1st LADY
Oh, I crave their pardon!—I remember the Names, but know nothing of the Story.

More **COMPANY** enters.

1st GENTLEMAN
Was not that Lady Frances Touchwood, coming up with Mrs. Racket?

2nd GENTLEMAN
I think so;—yes, it is, faith.—Let us go nearer.

Enter **LADY FRANCES**, **MRS RACKET**, and **MISS OGLE**.

SILVERTONGUE
Yes, Sir, this is to be the first Lot:—the Model of a City, in wax.

2nd GENTLEMAN
The Model of a City! What City?

SILVERTONGUE
That I have not been able to discover; but call it Rome, Pekin, or London, 'tis still a City: you'll find in it the same jarring interests, the same passions, the same virtues, and the same vices, whatever the name.

1st GENTLEMAN
You may as well present us a Map of Terra Incognita.

SILVERTONGUE
Oh, pardon me, Sir! a lively imagination would convert this waxen City into an endless and interesting amusement. For instance—look into this little House on the right-hand; there are four old Prudes in it, taking care of their Neighbours Reputations. This elegant Mansion on the left, decorated with Corinthian pillars—who needs be told that it belongs to a Court Lord, and is the habitation of Patriotism,

Philosophy, and Virtue? Here's a City Hall—the rich steams that issue from the windows, nourish a neighbouring Work-House. Here's a Church—we'll pass over that, the doors are shut. The Parsonage-house comes next;—we'll take a peep here, however.—Look at the Doctor! he's asleep on a volume of Toland; whilst his Lady is putting on rouge for the Masquerade.—Oh! oh! this can be no English City; our Parsons are all orthodox, and their Wives the daughters of Modesty and Meekness.

LADY FRANCES and **MISS OGLE** come forward, followed by **COURTALL**.

LADY FRANCES

I wish Sir George was here.—This man follows me about, and stares at me in such a way, that I am quite uneasy.

MISS OGLE

He has travell'd, and is heir to an immense estate; so he's impertinent by Patent.

COURTALL

You are very cruel, Ladies. Miss Ogle—you will not let me speak to you. As to this little scornful Beauty, she has frown'd me dead fifty times.

LADY FRANCES

Sir—I am a married Woman. (Confus'd.)

COURTALL

A married Woman! a good hint. (Aside.) 'Twould be a shame if such a charming Woman was not married. But I see you are a Daphne just come from your sheep, and your meadows; your crook, and your waterfalls. Pray now, who is the happy Damon, to whom you have vow'd eternal truth and constancy?

MISS OGLE

'Tis Lady Frances Touchwood, Mr. Courtall, to whom you are speaking.

COURTALL

Lady Frances! By Heaven, that's Saville's old flame. [Aside.] I beg your Ladyship's pardon. I ought to have believed that such beauty could belong only to your Name—a Name I have long been enamour'd of; because I knew it to be that of the finest Woman in the world.

MRS RACKET comes forward.

LADY FRANCES

[Apart.] My dear Mrs. Racket, I am so frighten'd! Here's a Man making love to me, though he knows I am married.

MRS RACKET

Oh, the sooner for that, my dear; don't mind him. Was you at the Cassino last night, Mr. Courtall?

COURTALL

I look'd in.—'Twas impossible to stay. No body there but Antiques. You'll be at Lady Brilliant's to-night, doubtless?

MRS RACKET

Yes, I go with Lady Frances.

LADY FRANCES

Bless me! I did not know this Gentleman was acquainted with Mrs. Racket.—I behaved so rude to him! [To **MISS OGLE.**]

MRS RACKET

Come, Ma'am; [looking at her Watch.] 'tis past one. I protest, if we don't fly to Kensington, we sha'n't find a soul there.

LADY FRANCES

Won't this Gentleman go with us?

COURTALL [Looking surpris'd.]

To be sure, you make me happy, Madam, beyond description.

MRS RACKET

Oh, never mind him—he'll follow.

[Exeunt **LADY FRANCES**, **MRS RACKET**, and **MISS OGLE.**

COURTALL

Lady Touchwood! with a vengeance! But, 'tis always so;—your reserved Ladies are like ice, 'egad!—no sooner begin to soften, than they melt.

[Following.

ACT III

SCENE I. Mr. Hardy's

Enter **LETITIA** and **MRS RACKET.**

MRS RACKET

Come, prepare, prepare; your Lover is coming.

LETITIA

My Lover!—Confess now that my absence at dinner was a severe mortification to him.

MRS RACKET

I can't absolutely swear it spoilt his appetite; he eat as if he was hungry, and drank his wine as though he liked it.

LETITIA

What was the apology?

MRS RACKET
That you were ill;—but I gave him a hint, that your extreme bashfulness could not support his eye.

LETITIA
If I comprehend him, aukwardness and bashfulness are the last faults he can pardon in a woman; so expect to see me transform'd into the veriest maukin.

MRS RACKET
You persevere then?

LETITIA
Certainly. I know the design is a rash one, and the event important;—it either makes Doricourt mine by all the tenderest ties of passion, or deprives me of him for ever; and never to be his wife will afflict me less, than to be his wife and not be belov'd.

MRS RACKET
So you wo'n't trust to the good old maxim—"Marry first, and love will follow?"

LETITIA
As readily as I would venture my last guinea, that good fortune might follow. The woman that has not touch'd the heart of a man before he leads her to the altar, has scarcely a chance to charm it when possession and security turn their powerful arms against her.—But here he comes.—I'll disappear for a moment.—Don't spare me.

[Exit **LETITIA**.

Enter **DORICOURT** (not seeing **MRS RACKET**.)

DORICOURT
So! [Looking at a Picture.] this is my mistress, I presume.—Ma foi! the painter has hit her off.—The downcast eye—the blushing cheek—timid—apprehensive—bashful.—A tear and a prayer-book would have made her La Bella Magdalena.—

Give me a woman in whose touching mien
A mind, a soul, a polish'd art is seen;
Whose motion speaks, whose poignant air can move.
Such are the darts to wound with endless love.

MRS RACKET
Is that an impromptu?

[Touching him on the shoulder with her fan.]

DORICOURT (starting.)
Madam!—[Aside.] Finely caught!—Not absolutely—it struck me during the dessert, as a motto for your picture.

MRS RACKET

Gallantly turn'd! I perceive, however, Miss Hardy's charms have made no violent impression on you.—And who can wonder?—the poor girl's defects are so obvious.

DORICOURT

Defects!

MRS RACKET

Merely those of education.—Her father's indulgence ruin'd her.—Mauvaise honte—conceit and ignorance—all unite in the Lady you are to marry.

DORICOURT

Marry!—I marry such a woman!—Your picture, I hope, is overcharged.—I marry mauvaise honte, pertness and ignorance!

MRS RACKET

Thank your stars, that ugliness and ill temper are not added to the list.—You must think her handsome?

DORICOURT

Half her personal beauty would content me; but could the Medicean Venus be animated for me, and endowed with a vulgar soul, I should become the statue, and my heart transformed to marble.

MRS RACKET

Bless us!—We are in a hopeful way then!

DORICOURT (Aside.)

There must be some envy in this!—I see she is a coquette. Ha, ha, ha! And you imagine I am persuaded of the truth of your character? ha, ha, ha! Miss Hardy, I have been assur'd, Madam, is elegant and accomplished:—but one must allow for a Lady's painting.

MRS RACKET (Aside.)

I'll be even with him for that. Ha! ha! ha! And so you have found me out!—Well, I protest I meant no harm; 'twas only to increase the éclat of her appearance, that I threw a veil over her charms.—Here comes the Lady;—her elegance and accomplishments will announce themselves.

Enter **LETITIA**, running.

LETITIA

La! Cousin, do you know that our John—oh, dear heart!—I didn't see you, Sir.

(Hanging down her head, and dropping behind **MRS RACKET**.)

MRS RACKET

Fye, Letitia! Mr. Doricourt thinks you a woman of elegant manners. Stand forward, and confirm his opinion.

LETITIA

No, no; keep before me.—He's my Sweetheart; and 'tis impudent to look one's Sweetheart in the face, you know.

MRS RACKET
You'll allow in future for a Lady's painting, Sir. Ha! ha! ha!

DORICOURT
I am astonish'd!

LETITIA
Well, hang it, I'll take heart.—Why, he is but a Man, you know, Cousin;—and I'll let him see I wasn't born in a Wood to be scar'd by an Owl. [Half apart; advances, and looks at him through her fingers.] He! he! he! [Goes up to him, and makes a very stiff formal curtesy.]—[He bows.]—You have been a great Traveller, Sir, I hear?

DORICOURT
Yes, Madam.

LETITIA
Then I wish you'd tell us about the fine sights you saw when you went over-sea.—I have read in a book, that there are some countries where the Men and Women are all Horses.—Did you see any of them?

MRS RACKET
Mr. Doricourt is not prepared, my dear, for these enquiries; he is reflecting on the importance of the question, and will answer you—when he can.

LETITIA
When he can! Why, he's as slow in speech, as Aunt Margery, when she's reading Thomas Aquinas;—and stands gaping like mum-chance.

MRS RACKET
Have a little discretion.

LETITIA
Hold your tongue!—Sure I may say what I please before I am married, if I can't afterwards.—D'ye think a body does not know how to talk to a Sweetheart. He is not the first I have had.

DORICOURT
Indeed!

LETITIA
Oh, Lud! He speaks!—Why, if you must know—there was the Curate at home:—when Papa was a-hunting, he used to come a suitoring, and make speeches to me out of books.—No body knows what a mort of fine things he used to say to me;—and call me Venis, and Jubah, and Dinah!

DORICOURT
And pray, fair Lady, how did you answer him?

LETITIA

Why, I used to say, Look you, Mr. Curate, don't think to come over me with your flim-flams; for a better Man than ever trod in your shoes, is coming over-sea to marry me;—but, ifags! I begin to think I was out.—Parson Dobbins was the sprightfuller man of the two.

DORICOURT

Surely this cannot be Miss Hardy!

LETITIA

Laws! why, don't you know me! You saw me to-day—but I was daunted before my Father, and the Lawyer, and all them, and did not care to speak out:—so, may be, you thought I couldn't;—but I can talk as fast as any body, when I know folks a little:—and now I have shewn my parts, I hope you'll like me better.

Enter **MR HARDY**.

MR HARDY

I foresee this won't do!—Mr. Doricourt, may be you take my Daughter for a Fool; but you are mistaken: she's a sensible Girl, as any in England.

DORICOURT

I am convinced she has a very uncommon understanding, Sir. [Aside.] I did not think he had been such an Ass.

LETITIA

My Father will undo the whole.—Laws! Papa, how can you think he can take me for a fool! when every body knows I beat the Potecary at Conundrums last Christmas-time? and didn't I make a string of names, all in riddles, for the Lady's Diary?—There was a little River, and a great House; that was Newcastle.—There was what a Lamb says, and three Letters; that was Ba, and k-e-r, ker, Baker. —There was—

MR HARDY

Don't stand ba-a-ing there. You'll make me mad in a moment!—I tell you, Sir, that for all that, she's dev'lish sensible.

DORICOURT

Sir, I give all possible credit to your assertions.

LETITIA

Laws! Papa, do come along. If you stand watching, how can my Sweetheart break his mind, and tell me how he admires me?

DORICOURT

That would be difficult, indeed, Madam.

MR HARDY

I tell you, Letty, I'll have no more of this.—I see well enough—

LETITIA

Laws! don't snub me before my Husband—that is to be.—You'll teach him to snub me too,—and I believe, by his looks, he'd like to begin now.—So, let us go, Cousin; you may tell the Gentleman what a genus I have—how I can cut Watch-papers, and work Cat-gut; make Quadrille-baskets with Pins, and take Profiles in Shade; ay, as well as the Lady at No. 62, South Moulton-street, Grosvenor-square.

[Exit **MR HARDY** and **LETITIA**.

MRS RACKET

What think you of my painting, now?

DORICOURT

Oh, mere water-colours, Madam! The Lady has caricatured your picture.

MRS RACKET

And how does she strike you on the whole?

DORICOURT

Like a good Design, spoiled by the incapacity of the Artist. Her faults are evidently the result of her Father's weak indulgence. I observed an expression in her eye, that seemed to satyrise the folly of her lips.

MRS RACKET

But at her age, when Education is fixed, and Manner becomes Nature—hopes of improvement—

DORICOURT

Would be as rational, as hopes of Gold from a Jugler's Crucible.—Doricourt's Wife must be incapable of improvement; but it must be because she's got beyond it.

MRS RACKET

I am pleased your misfortune sits no heavier.

DORICOURT

Your pardon, Madam; so mercurial was the hour in which I was born, that misfortunes always go plump to the bottom of my heart, like a pebble in water, and leave the surface unruffled.—I shall certainly set off for Bath, or the other world, to-night;—but whether I shall use a chaise with four swift coursers, or go off in a tangent—from the aperture of a pistol, deserves consideration; so I make my adieus.

(Going.)

MRS RACKET

Oh, but I intreat you, postpone your journey 'till to-morrow; determine on which you will—you must be this night at the Masquerade.

DORICOURT

Masquerade!

MRS RACKET

Why not?—If you resolve to visit the other world, you may as well take one night's pleasure first in this, you know.

DORICOURT
Faith, that's very true; Ladies are the best Philosophers, after all. Expect me at the Masquerade.

[Exit **DORICOURT**.

MRS RACKET
He's a charming Fellow!—I think Letitia sha'n't have him.

(Going.)

Enter **MR HARDY**.

MR HARDY
What's he gone?

MRS RACKET
Yes; and I am glad he is. You would have ruined us!—Now, I beg, Mr. Hardy, you won't interfere in this business; it is a little out of your way.

[Exit **MRS RACKET**.

MR HARDY
Hang me, if I don't though. I foresee very clearly what will be the end of it, if I leave ye to yourselves; so, I'll e'en follow him to the Masquerade, and tell him all about it: Let me see.—What shall my dress be? A Great Mogul? No.—A Grenadier? No;—no, that, I foresee, would make a laugh. Hang me, if I don't send to my favourite little Quick, and borrow his Jew Isaac's dress:—I know the Dog likes a glass of good wine; so I'll give him a bottle of my Forty-eight, and he shall teach me. Aye, that's it—I'll be Cunning Little Isaac! If they complain of my want of wit, I'll tell 'em the cursed Duenna wears the breeches, and has spoilt my parts.

[Exit **HARDY**.

SCENE II.—Courtall's

Enter **COURTALL, SAVILLE**, and three **OTHERS**, from an Apartment in the back Scene. (The last three tipsey.)

COURTALL
You shan't go yet:—Another catch, and another bottle!

1st GENTLEMAN
May I be a bottle, and an empty bottle, if you catch me at that!—Why, I am going to the Masquerade. Jack—, you know who I mean, is to meet me, and we are to have a leap at the new lustres.

2nd GENTLEMAN

And I am going too—a Harlequin—(hiccups) Am not I in a pretty pickle to make Harlequinades?—And Tony, here—he is going in the disguise—in the disguise—of a Gentleman!

1st GENTLEMAN

We are all very disguised; so bid them draw up—D'ye hear!

[Exeunt the three **GENTLEMEN**.

SAVILLE

Thy skull, Courtall, is a Lady's thimble:—no, an egg-shell.

COURTALL

Nay, then you are gone too; you never aspire to similes, but in your cups.

SAVILLE

No, no; I am steady enough—but the fumes of the wine pass directly through thy egg-shell, and leave thy brain as cool as—Hey! I am quite sober; my similes fail me.

COURTALL

Then we'll sit down here, and have one sober bottle.—Bring a table and glasses.

SAVILLE

I'll not swallow another drop; no, though the juice should be the true Falernian.

COURTALL

By the bright eyes of her you love, you shall drink her health.

SAVILLE

Ah! (sitting down.) Her I loved is gone (sighing.)—She's married!

COURTALL

Then bless your stars you are not her Husband! I would be Husband to no Woman in Europe, who was not dev'lish rich, and dev'lish ugly.

SAVILLE

Wherefore ugly?

COURTALL

Because she could not have the conscience to exact those attentions that a Pretty Wife expects; or, if she should, her resentments would be perfectly easy to me, nobody would undertake to revenge her cause.

SAVILLE

Thou art a most licentious fellow!

COURTALL

I should hate my own wife, that's certain; but I have a warm heart for those of other people; and so here's to the prettiest Wife in England—Lady Frances Touchwood.

SAVILLE
Lady Frances Touchwood! I rise to drink her. (drinks) How the devil came Lady Frances in your head? I never knew you give a Woman of Chastity before.

COURTALL
That's odd, for you have heard me give half the Women of Fashion in England.—But, pray now, what do you take a Woman of Chastity to be? (sneeringly.)

SAVILLE
Such a woman as Lady Frances Touchwood, Sir.

COURTALL
Oh, you are grave, Sir; I remember you was an Adorer of her's—Why didn't you marry her?

SAVILLE
I had not the arrogance to look so high—Had my fortune been worthy of her, she should not have been ignorant of my admiration.

COURTALL
Precious fellow! What, I suppose you would not dare tell her now that you admire her?

SAVILLE
No, nor you.

COURTALL
By the Lord, I have told her so.

SAVILLE
Have! Impossible!

COURTALL
Ha! ha! ha!—Is it so?

SAVILLE
How did she receive the declaration?

COURTALL
Why, in the old way; blushed, and frowned, and said she was married.

SAVILLE
What amazing things thou art capable of! I could more easily have taken the Pope by the beard, than prophaned her ears with such a declaration.

COURTALL

I shall meet her at Lady Brilliant's to-night, where I shall repeat it; and I'll lay my life, under a mask, she'll hear it all without blush, or frown.

SAVILLE (rising)
'Tis false, Sir!—She won't.

COURTALL
She will! (rising) Nay, I'd venture to lay a round sum, that I prevail on her to go out with me—only to taste the fresh air, I mean.

SAVILLE
Preposterous vanity! From this moment I suspect that half the victories you have boasted, are false and slanderous, as your pretended influence with Lady Frances.

COURTALL
Pretended!—How should such a Fellow as you, now, who never soared beyond a cherry-cheeked Daughter of a Ploughman in Norfolk, judge of the influence of a Man of my Figure and Habits? I could shew thee a list, in which there are names to shake thy faith in the whole sex!—and, to that list I have no doubt of adding the name of Lady—

SAVILLE
Hold, Sir! My ears cannot bear the profanation;—you cannot—dare not approach her!—For your soul you dare not mention Love to her! Her look would freeze the word, whilst it hovered on thy licentious lips!

COURTALL
Whu! whu! Well, we shall see—this evening, by Jupiter, the trial shall be made—if I fail—I fail.

SAVILLE
I think thou darest not!—But my life, my honour on her purity.

[Exit **SAVILLE**.

COURTALL
Hot-headed fool! But since he has brought it to this point, by Gad I'll try what can be done with her Ladyship (musing)—(rings) She's frost-work, and the prejudices of education yet strong: ergo, passionate professions will only inflame her pride, and put her on her guard.—For other arts then!

Enter **DICK**.

Dick, do you know any of the servants at Sir George Touchwood's?

DICK
Yes, Sir; I knows the Groom, and one of the House-maids: for the matter-o'-that, she's my own Cousin; and it was my Mother that help'd her to the place.

COURTALL
Do you know Lady Frances's Maid?

DICK

I can't say as how I know she.

COURTALL

Do you know Sir George's Valet?

DICK

No, Sir; but Sally is very thick with Mr. Gibson, Sir George's Gentleman.

COURTALL

Then go there directly, and employ Sally to discover whether her Master goes to Lady Brilliant's this evening; and, if he does, the name of the shop that sold his Habit.

DICK

Yes, Sir.

COURTALL

Be exact in your intelligence, and come to me at Boodle's:

[Exit **DICK**.]

If I cannot otherwise succeed, I'll beguile her as Jove did Alcmena, in the shape of her Husband. The possession of so fine a Woman—the triumph over Saville, are each a sufficient motive; and united, they shall be resistless.

[Exit **COURTALL**.

SCENE III.—The Street

Enter **SAVILLE**.

SAVILLE

The air has recover'd me! What have I been doing! Perhaps my petulance may be the cause of her ruin, whose honour I asserted:—his vanity is piqued;—and where Women are concerned, Courtall can be a villain.

Enter **DICK**. Bows, and passes hastily.

Ha! that's his Servant!—Dick!

DICK [returning]
Sir.

SAVILLE
Where are you going, Dick?

DICK

Going! I am going, Sir, where my Master sent me.

SAVILLE

Well answer'd;—but I have a particular reason for my enquiry, and you must tell me.

DICK

Why then, Sir, I am going to call upon a Cousin of mine, that lives at Sir George Touchwood's.

SAVILLE

Very well.—There, [gives him money] you must make your Cousin drink my health.—What are you going about?

DICK

Why, Sir, I believe 'tis no harm, or elseways I am sure I would not blab.—I am only going to ax if Sir George goes to the Masquerade to-night, and what Dress he wears.

SAVILLE

Enough! Now, Dick, if you will call at my lodgings in your way back, and acquaint me with your Cousin's intelligence, I'll double the trifle I have given you.

DICK

Bless your honour, I'll call—never fear.

[Exit **DICK**.

SAVILLE

Surely the occasion may justify the means:—'tis doubly my duty to be Lady Frances's Protector. Courtall, I see, is planning an artful scheme; but Saville shall out-plot him.

[Exit **SAVILLE**.

SCENE IV.—Sir George Touchwood's

Enter **SIR GEORGE** and **VILLERS**.

VILLERS

For shame, Sir George! you have left Lady Frances in tears.—How can you afflict her?

SIR GEORGE

'Tis I that am afflicted;—my dream of happiness is over.—Lady Frances and I are disunited.

VILLERS

The Devil! Why, you have been in town but ten days: she can have made no acquaintance for a Commons affair yet.

SIR GEORGE

Pho! 'tis our minds that are disunited: she no longer places her whole delight in me; she has yielded herself up to the world!

VILLERS

Yielded herself up to the World! Why did you not bring her to town in a Cage? Then she might have taken a peep at the World!—But, after all, what has the World done? A twelvemonth since you was the gayest fellow in it:—If any body ask'd who dresses best?—Sir George Touchwood.—Who is the most gallant Man? Sir George Touchwood.—Who is the most wedded to Amusement and Dissipation? Sir George Touchwood.—And now Sir George is metamorphosed into a sour Censor; and talks of Fashionable Life with as much bitterness, as the old crabbed Fellow in Rome.

SIR GEORGE

The moment I became possessed of such a jewel as Lady Frances, every thing wore a different complexion: that Society in which I liv'd with so much éclat, became the object of my terror; and I think of the manners of Polite Life, as I do of the atmosphere of a Pest-house.—My Wife is already infected; she was set upon this morning by Maids, Widows, and Bachelors, who carried her off in triumph, in spite of my displeasure.

VILLERS

Aye, to be sure; there would have been no triumph in the case, if you had not oppos'd it:—but I have heard the whole story from Mrs. Racket; and I assure you, Lady Frances didn't enjoy the morning at all;—she wish'd for you fifty times.

SIR GEORGE

Indeed! Are you sure of that?

VILLERS

Perfectly sure.

SIR GEORGE

I wish I had known it:—my uneasiness at dinner was occasioned by very different ideas.

VILLERS

Here then she comes, to receive your apology; but if she is true Woman, her displeasure will rise in proportion to your contrition;—and till you grow careless about her pardon, she won't grant it:—however, I'll leave you.—Matrimonial Duets are seldom set in the style I like.

[Exit **VILLERS**.

Enter **LADY FRANCES**.

SIR GEORGE

The sweet sorrow that glitters in these eyes, I cannot bear (embracing her). Look chearfully, you Rogue.

LADY FRANCES

I cannot look otherwise, if you are pleas'd with me.

SIR GEORGE

Well, Fanny, to-day you made your entrée in the Fashionable World; tell me honestly the impressions you receiv'd.

LADY FRANCES

Indeed, Sir George, I was so hurried from place to place, that I had not time to find out what my impressions were.

SIR GEORGE

That's the very spirit of the life you have chosen.

LADY FRANCES

Every body about me seem'd happy—but every body seem'd in a hurry to be happy somewhere else.

SIR GEORGE

And you like this?

LADY FRANCES

One must like what the rest of the World likes.

SIR GEORGE

Pernicious maxim!

LADY FRANCES

But, my dear Sir George, you have not promis'd to go with me to the Masquerade.

SIR GEORGE

'Twould be a shocking indecorum to be seen together, you know.

LADY FRANCES

Oh, no; I ask'd Mrs. Racket, and she told me we might be seen together at the Masquerade—without being laugh'd at.

SIR GEORGE

Really?

LADY FRANCES

Indeed, to tell you the truth, I could wish it was the fashion for married people to be inseparable; for I have more heart-felt satisfaction in fifteen minutes with you at my side, than fifteen days of amusement could give me without you.

SIR GEORGE

My sweet Creature! How that confession charms me!—Let us begin the Fashion.

LADY FRANCES

O, impossible! We should not gain a single proselyte; and you can't conceive what spiteful things would be said of us.—At Kensington to-day a Lady met us, whom we saw at Court, when we were presented;

she lifted up her hands in amazement!—Bless me! said she to her companion, here's Lady Francis without Sir Hurlo Thrumbo!—My dear Mrs. Racket, consider what an important charge you have! For Heaven's sake take her home again, or some Enchanter on a flying Dragon will descend and carry her off.—Oh, said another, I dare say Lady Frances has a clue at her heel, like the peerless Rosamond:—her tender swain would never have trusted her so far without such a precaution.

SIR GEORGE
Heav'n and Earth!—How shall Innocence preserve its lustre amidst manners so corrupt!—My dear Fanny, I feel a sentiment for thee at this moment, tenderer than Love—more animated than Passion.—I could weep over that purity, expos'd to the sullying breath of Fashion, and the Ton, in whose latitudinary vortex Chastity herself can scarcely move unspotted.

Enter **GIBSON**.

GIBSON
Your Honour talk'd, I thought, something about going to the Masquerade?

SIR GEORGE
Well.

GIBSON
Isn't it?—hasn't your Honour?—I thought your Honour had forgot to order a Dress.

LADY FRANCES
Well consider'd, Gibson.—Come, will you be Jew, Turk, or Heretic; a Chinese Emperor, or a Ballad-Singer; a Rake, or a Watchman?

SIR GEORGE
Oh, neither, my Love; I can't take the trouble to support a character.

LADY FRANCES
You'll wear a Domino then:—I saw a pink Domino trimm'd with blue at the shop where I bought my Habit.—Would you like it?

SIR GEORGE
Any thing, any thing.

LADY FRANCES
Then go about it directly, Gibson.—A pink Domino trimm'd with blue, and a Hat of the same—Come, you have not seen my Dress yet—it is most beautiful; I long to have it on.

[Exeunt **SIR GEORGE** and **LADY FRANCES**.

GIBSON
A pink Domino trimm'd with blue, and a Hat of the same—What the devil can it signify to Sally now what his Dress is to be?—Surely the Slut has not made an assignation to meet her Master!

[Exit **GIBSON**.

ACT IV

SCENE I.—A Masquerade

A Party dancing Cotillons in front—a variety of Characters pass and repass.

Enter **FOLLY** on a Hobby-Horse, with Cap and Bells.

MASK
Hey! Tom Fool! what business have you here?

FOLLY
What, Sir! Affront a Prince in his own Dominions!

[Struts off.

MOUNTEBANK
Who'll buy my Nostrums? Who'll buy my Nostrums?

MASK
What are they?

(They all come round him.)

MOUNTEBANK
Different sorts, and for different customers. Here's a Liquor for Ladies—it expels the rage of Gaming and Gallantry; Here's a Pill for Members of Parliament—good to settle Consciences. Here's an Eye-Water for Jealous Husbands—it thickens the Visual Membrane, through which they see too clearly. Here's a Decoction for the Clergy—it never sits easy, if the patient has more than One Living. Here's a Draught for Lawyers—a great promoter of Modesty. Here's a Powder for Projectors—'twill rectify the fumes of an Empty Stomach, and dissipate their airy castles.

MASK
Have you a Nostrum that can give patience to Young Heirs, whose Uncles and Fathers are stout and healthy?

MOUNTEBANK
Yes; and I have an Infusion for Creditors—it gives resignation and humility, when Fine Gentlemen break their promises, or plead their privilege.

MASK
Come along:—I'll find you customers for your whole cargo.

Enter **MR HARDY**, in the Dress of Isaac Mendoza.

MR HARDY

Why, isn't it a shame to see so many stout, well-built Young Fellows, masquerading, and cutting Couranta's here at home—instead of making the French cut capers to the tune of your Cannon—or sweating the Spaniards with an English Fandango?—I foresee the end of all this.

MASK

Why, thou little testy Israelite! back to Duke's Place; and preach your tribe into a subscription for the good of the land on whose milk and honey ye fatten.—Where are your Joshuas and your Gideons, aye? What! all dwindled into Stockbrokers, Pedlars, and Rag-Men?

MR HARDY

No, not all. Some of us turn Christians, and by degrees grow into all the privileges of Englishmen! In the second generation we are Patriots, Rebels, Courtiers, and Husbands.

[Puts his fingers to his forehead.]

Two other **MASKS** advance.

3d MASK

What, my little Isaac!—How the Devil came you here? Where's your old Margaret?

MR HARDY

Oh, I have got rid of her.

3d MASK

How?

MR HARDY

Why, I persuaded a young Irishman that she was a blooming plump Beauty of eighteen; so they made an Elopement, ha! ha! ha! and she is now the Toast of Tipperary. Ha! there's Cousin Racket and her Party; they sha'n't know me.

[Puts on his Mask.

Enter **MRS RACKET**, **LADY FRANCES**, **SIR GEORGE**, and **FLUTTER**.

MRS RACKET

Look at this dumpling Jew; he must be a Levïte by his figure. You have surely practised the flesh-hook a long time, friend, to have raised that goodly presence.

MR HARDY

About as long, my brisk Widow, as you have been angling for a second Husband; but my hook has been better baited than your's.—You have only caught Gudgeons, I see.

[Pointing to **FLUTTER**.

FLUTTER

Oh! this is one of the Geniuses they hire to entertain the Company with their accidental sallies.—Let me look at your Common-Place Book, friend.—I want a few good things.

MR HARDY
I'd oblige you, with all my heart; but you'll spoil them in repeating—or, if you shou'd not, they'll gain you no reputation—for no body will believe they are your own.

SIR GEORGE
He knows ye, Flutter;—the little Gentleman fancies himself a Wit, I see.

MR HARDY
There's no depending on what you see—the eyes of the jealous are not to be trusted.—Look to your Lady.

FLUTTER
He knows ye, Sir George.

SIR GEORGE
What! am I the Town-talk? [Aside]

MR HARDY
I can neither see Doricourt nor Letty.—I must find them out.

[Exit **MR HARDY**.

MRS RACKET
Well, Lady Frances, is not all this charming? Could you have conceived such a brilliant assemblage of objects?

LADY FRANCES
Delightful! The days of enchantment are restor'd; the columns glow with Sapphires and Rubies. Emperors and Fairies, Beauties and Dwarfs, meet me at every step.

SIR GEORGE
How lively are first impressions on sensible minds! In four hours, vapidity and languor will take place of that exquisite sense of joy, which flutters your little heart.

MRS RACKET
What an inhuman creature! Fate has not allow'd us these sensations above ten times in our lives; and would you have us shorten them by anticipation?

FLUTTER
O Lord! your Wise Men are the greatest Fools upon earth:—they reason about their enjoyments, and analyse their pleasures, whilst the essence escapes. Look, Lady Frances: D'ye see that Figure strutting in the dress of an Emperor? His Father retails Oranges in Botolph Lane. That Gypsey is a Maid of Honour, and that Rag-man a Physician.

LADY FRANCES

Why, you know every body.

FLUTTER

Oh, every creature.—A Mask is nothing at all to me.—I can give you the history of half the people here. In the next apartment there's a whole family, who, to my knowledge, have lived on Water-Cresses this month, to make a figure here to-night;—but, to make up for that, they'll cram their pockets with cold Ducks and Chickens, for a Carnival to-morrow.

LADY FRANCES

Oh, I should like to see this provident Family.

FLUTTER

Honour me with your arm.

[Exeunt **FLUTTER** and **LADY FRANCES**.

MRS RACKET

Come, Sir George, you shall be my Beau.—We'll make the tour of the rooms, and meet them. Oh! your pardon, you must follow Lady Frances; or the wit and fine parts of Mr. Flutter may drive you out of her head. Ha! ha! ha!

[Exit **MRS RACKET**.

SIR GEORGE

I was going to follow her, and now I dare not. How can I be such a fool as to be govern'd by the fear of that ridicule which I despise!

[Exit **SIR GEORGE**.

Enter **DORICOURT**, meeting a **MASK**.

DORICOURT

Ha! my Lord!—I thought you had been engaged at Westminster on this important night.

MASK

So I am—I slipt out as soon as Lord Trope got upon his legs; I can badinage here an hour or two, and be back again before he is down.—There's a fine Figure! I'll address her.

Enter **LETITIA**.

Charity, fair Lady! Charity for a poor Pilgrim.

LETITIA

Charity! If you mean my prayers, Heaven grant thee Wit, Pilgrim.

MASK

That blessing would do from a Devotee: from you I ask other charities;—such charities as Beauty should bestow—soft Looks—sweet Words—and kind Wishes.

LETITIA

Alas! I am bankrupt of these, and forced to turn Beggar myself.—There he is!—how shall I catch his attention?

MASK

Will you grant me no favour?

LETITIA

Yes, one—I'll make you my Partner—not for life, but through the soft mazes of a minuet.—Dare you dance?

DORICOURT

Some spirit in that.

MASK

I dare do any thing you command.

DORICOURT

Do you know her, my Lord?

MASK

No: Such a woman as that, would formerly have been known in any disguise; but Beauty is now common—Venus seems to have given her Cestus to the whole sex.

A Minuet.

DORICOURT (during the Minuet)
She dances divinely.—(When ended)
Somebody must know her! Let us enquire who she is.

[Exit.

Enter **SAVILLE** and **KITTY WILLIS**, habited like **LADY FRANCES**.

SAVILLE

I have seen Courtall in Sir George's habit, though he endeavoured to keep himself conceal'd. Go, and seat yourself in the tea-room, and on no account discover your face:—remember too, Kitty, that the Woman you are to personate is a Woman of Virtue.

KITTY

I am afraid I shall find that a difficult character: indeed I believe it is seldom kept up through a whole Masquerade.

SAVILLE

Of that you can be no judge—Follow my directions, and you shall be rewarded. [Exit Kitty.

Enter **DORICOURT**.

DORICOURT

Ha! Saville! Did you see a Lady dance just now?

SAVILLE

No.

DORICOURT

Very odd. No body knows her.

SAVILLE

Where is Miss Hardy?

DORICOURT

Cutting Watch-papers, and making Conundrums, I suppose.

SAVILLE

What do you mean?

DORICOURT

Faith, I hardly know. She's not here, however, Mrs. Racket tells me.—I ask'd no further.

SAVILLE

Your indifference seems increas'd.

DORICOURT

Quite the reverse; 'tis advanced thirty-two degrees towards hatred.

SAVILLE

You are jesting?

DORICOURT

Then it must be with a very ill grace, my dear Saville; for I never felt so seriously: Do you know the creature's almost an Ideot?

SAVILLE

What!

DORICOURT

An Ideot. What the devil shall I do with her? Egad! I think I'll feign myself mad—and then Hardy will propose to cancel the engagements.

SAVILLE

An excellent expedient. I must leave you; you are mysterious, and I can't stay to unravel ye.—I came here to watch over Innocence and Beauty.

DORICOURT

The Guardian of Innocence and Beauty at three and twenty! Is there not a cloven foot under that black gown, Saville?

SAVILLE
No, faith. Courtall is here on a most detestable design.—I found means to get a knowledge of the Lady's dress, and have brought a girl to personate her, whose reputation cannot be hurt.—You shall know the result to-morrow. Adieu.

[Exit **SAVILLE**.

DORICOURT (musing)
Yes, I think that will do.—I'll feign myself mad, see the Doctor to pronounce me incurable, and when the parchments are destroyed—

[As he stands in a musing posture, **LETITIA** enters, and sings.]

SONG.
Wake! thou Son of Dullness, wake!
From thy drowsy senses shake
All the spells that Care employs,
Cheating Mortals of their joys.

II.
Light-wing'd Spirits, hither haste!
Who prepare for mortal taste
All the gifts that Pleasure sends,
Every bliss that youth attends.

III.
Touch his feelings, rouze his soul,
Whilst the sparkling moments roll;
Bid them wake to new delight,
Crown the magic of the night.

DORICOURT
By Heaven, the same sweet creature!

LETITIA
You have chosen an odd situation for study. Fashion and Taste preside in this spot:—they throw their spells around you:—ten thousand delights spring up at their command;—and you, a Stoic—a being without senses, are wrapt in reflection.

DORICOURT
And you, the most charming being in the world, awake me to admiration. Did you come from the Stars?

LETITIA
Yes, and I shall reascend in a moment.

DORICOURT

Pray shew me your face before you go.

LETITIA

Beware of imprudent curiosity; it lost Paradise.

DORICOURT

Eve's curiosity was rais'd by the Devil;—'tis an Angel tempts mine.—So your allusion is not in point.

LETITIA

But why would you see my face?

DORICOURT

To fall in love with it.

LETITIA

And what then?

DORICOURT

Why, then—Aye, curse it! there's the rub. [Aside.]

LETITIA

Your Mistress will be angry;—but, perhaps, you have no Mistress?

DORICOURT

Yes, yes; and a sweet one it is!

LETITIA

What! is she old?

DORICOURT

No.

LETITIA

Ugly?

DORICOURT

No.

LETITIA

What then?

DORICOURT

Pho! don't talk about her; but shew me your face.

LETITIA

My vanity forbids it;—'twould frighten you.

DORICOURT

Impossible! Your Shape is graceful, your Air bewitching, your Bosom transparent, and your Chin would tempt me to kiss it, if I did not see a pouting red Lip above it, that demands—

LETITIA

You grow too free.

DORICOURT

Shew me your face then—only half a glance.

LETITIA

Not for worlds.

DORICOURT

What! you will have a little gentle force?

[Attempts to seize her Mask.

LETITIA

I am gone for ever!

[Exit.

DORICOURT

'Tis false;—I'll follow to the end.

[Exit.

FLUTTER, **LADY FRANCES**, and **SAVILLE** advance.

LADY FRANCES

How can you be thus interested for a stranger?

SAVILLE

Goodness will ever interest; its home is Heaven: on earth 'tis but a Wanderer. Imprudent Lady! why have you left the side of your Protector? Where is your Husband?

FLUTTER

Why, what's that to him?

LADY FRANCES

Surely it can't be merely his habit;—there's something in him that awes me.

FLUTTER

Pho! 'tis only his grey beard.—I know him; he keeps a Lottery-office on Cornhill.

SAVILLE

My province, as an Enchanter, lays open every secret to me. Lady! there are dangers abroad—Beware!

[Exit.

LADY FRANCES
'Tis very odd; his manner has made me tremble. Let us seek Sir George.

FLUTTER
He is coming towards us.

COURTALL comes forward, habited like **SIR GEORGE**.

COURTALL
There she is! If I can but disengage her from that fool Flutter—crown me, ye Schemers, with immortal wreaths.

LADY FRANCES
O my dear Sir George! I rejoice to meet you—an old Conjuror has been frightening me with his Prophecies.—Where's Mrs. Racket?

COURTALL
In the dancing-room.—I promis'd to send you to her, Mr. Flutter.

FLUTTER
Ah! she wants me to dance. With all my heart.

[Exit.

LADY FRANCES
Why do you keep on your mask?—'tis too warm.

COURTALL
'Tis very warm—I want air—let us go.

LADY FRANCES
You seem quite agitated.—Sha'n't we bid our company adieu?

COURTALL
No, no;—there's no time for forms. I'll just give directions to the carriage, and be with you in a moment. (Going, steps back.) Put on your mask; I have a particular reason for it.

[Exit.

SAVILLE advances with **KITTY**.

SAVILLE
Now, Kitty, you know your lesson. Lady Frances, (takes off his mask) let me lead you to your Husband.

LADY FRANCES

Heavens! is Mr. Saville the Conjuror? Sir George is just stept to the door to give directions.—We are going home immediately.

SAVILLE
No, Madam, you are deceiv'd: Sir George is this way.

LADY FRANCES
This is astonishing!

SAVILLE
Be not alarm'd: you have escap'd a snare, and shall be in safety in a moment.

[Exit **SAVILLE** and **LADY FRANCES**.

Enter **COURTALL**, and seizes **KITTY'S** Hand.

COURTALL
Now!

KITTY
'Tis pity to go so soon.

COURTALL
Perhaps I may bring you back, my Angel—but go now, you must.

[Exit.]

[Music.]

DORICOURT and **LETITIA** come forward.

DORICOURT
By Heavens! I never was charm'd till now.—English beauty—French vivacity—wit—elegance. Your name, my Angel!—tell me your name, though you persist in concealing your face.

LETITIA
My name has a spell in it.

DORICOURT
I thought so; it must be Charming.

LETITIA
But if reveal'd, the charm is broke.

DORICOURT
I'll answer for its force.

LETITIA

Suppose it Harriet, or Charlotte, or Maria, or—

DORICOURT
Hang Harriet, and Charlotte, and Maria—the name your Father gave ye!

LETITIA
That can't be worth knowing, 'tis so transient a thing.

DORICOURT
How, transient?

LETITIA
Heav'n forbid my name should be lasting till I am married.

DORICOURT
Married! The chains of Matrimony are too heavy and vulgar for such a spirit as yours.—The flowery wreaths of Cupid are the only bands you should wear.

LETITIA
They are the lightest, I believe: but 'tis possible to wear those of Marriage gracefully.—Throw 'em loosely round, and twist 'em in a True-Lover's Knot for the Bosom.

DORICOURT
An Angel! But what will you be when a Wife?

LETITIA
A Woman.—If my Husband should prove a Churl, a Fool, or a Tyrant, I'd break his heart, ruin his fortune, elope with the first pretty Fellow that ask'd me—and return the contempt of the world with scorn, whilst my feelings prey'd upon my life.

DORICOURT
Amazing! [Aside] What if you lov'd him, and he were worthy of your love?

LETITIA
Why, then I'd be any thing—and all!—Grave, gay, capricious—the soul of whim, the spirit of variety—live with him in the eye of fashion, or in the shade of retirement—change my country, my sex,—feast with him in an Esquimaux hut, or a Persian pavilion—join him in the victorious war-dance on the borders of Lake Ontario, or sleep to the soft breathings of the flute in the cinnamon groves of Ceylon —dig with him in the mines of Golconda, or enter the dangerous precincts of the Mogul's Seraglo—cheat him of his wishes, and overturn his empire to restore the Husband of my Heart to the blessings of Liberty and Love.

DORICOURT
Delightful wildness! Oh, to catch thee, and hold thee for ever in this little cage!

[Attempting to clasp her.

LETITIA

Hold, Sir! Though Cupid must give the bait that tempts me to the snare, 'tis Hymen must spread the net to catch me.

DORICOURT
'Tis in vain to assume airs of coldness—Fate has ordain'd you mine.

LETITIA
How do you know?

DORICOURT
I feel it here. I never met with a Woman so perfectly to my taste; and I won't believe it form'd you so, on purpose to tantalize me.

LETITIA
This moment is worth a whole existence. [Aside.]

DORICOURT
Come, shew me your face, and rivet my chains.

LETITIA
To-morrow you shall be satisfied.

DORICOURT
To-morrow! and not to-night?

LETITIA
No.

DORICOURT
Where then shall I wait on you to-morrow?—Where see you?

LETITIA
You shall see me in an hour when you least expect me.

DORICOURT
Why all this mystery?

LETITIA
I like to be mysterious. At present be content to know that I am a Woman of Family and Fortune. Adieu!

Enter **MR HARDY**.

MR HARDY
Adieu! Then I am come at the fag end. [Aside.]

DORICOURT
Let me see you to your carriage.

LETITIA

As you value knowing me, stir not a step. If I am follow'd, you never see me more.

[Exit.

DORICOURT

Barbarous Creature! She's gone! What, and is this really serious?—am I in love?—Pho! it can't be—O Flutter! do you know that charming Creature?

Enter **FLUTTER**.

FLUTTER

What charming Creature? I pass'd a thousand.

DORICOURT

She went out at that door, as you enter'd.

FLUTTER

Oh, yes;—I know her very well.

DORICOURT

Do you, my dear Fellow? Who?

FLUTTER

She's kept by Lord George Jennett.

MR HARDY

Impudent Scoundrel! [Aside.]

DORICOURT

Kept!!!

FLUTTER

Yes; Colonel Gorget had her first;—then Mr. Loveill;—then—I forget exactly how many; and at last she's Lord George's.

[Talks to other **MASKS.**]

DORICOURT

I'll murder Gorget, poison Lord George, and shoot myself.

MR HARDY

Now's the time, I see, to clear up the whole. Mr. Doricourt!—I say—Flutter was mistaken; I know who you are in love with.

DORICOURT

A strange rencontre! Who?

MR HARDY
My Letty.

DORICOURT
Oh! I understand your rebuke;—'tis too soon, Sir, to assume the Father-in-law.

MR HARDY
Zounds! what do you mean by that? I tell you that the Lady you admire, is Letitia Hardy.

DORICOURT
I am glad you are so well satisfied with the state of my heart.—I wish I was.

[Exit.

MR HARDY
Stop a moment.—Stop, I say! What, you won't? Very well—if I don't play you a trick for this, may I never be a Grand-father! I'll plot with Letty now, and not against her; aye, hang me if I don't. There's something in my head, that shall tingle in his heart.—He shall have a lecture upon impatience, that I foresee he'll be the better for as long as he lives.

[Exit.

SAVILLE comes forward with other **MASKS**.

SAVILLE
Flutter, come with us; we're going to raise a laugh at Courtall's.

FLUTTER
With all my heart. "Live to Live," was my Father's motto: "Live to Laugh," is mine.

[Exit.

SCENE II.—Courtall's

Enter **KITTY** and **COURTALL**.

KITTY
Where have you brought me, Sir George? This is not our home.

COURTALL
'Tis my home, beautiful Lady Frances!

[Kneels, and takes off his Mask.]

Oh, forgive the ardency of my passion, which has compell'd me to deceive you.

KITTY
Mr. Courtall! what will become of me?

COURTALL
Oh, say but that you pardon the Wretch who adores you. Did you but know the agonizing tortures of my heart, since I had the felicity of conversing with you this morning—or the despair that now—

[Knock.]

KITTY
Oh! I'm undone!

COURTALL
Zounds! my dear Lady Frances. I am not at home. Rascal! do you hear?—Let no body in; I am not at home.

SERVANT [Without]
Sir, I told the Gentlemen so.

COURTALL
Eternal curses! they are coming up. Step into this room, adorable Creature! one moment; I'll throw them out of the window if they stay three.

[Exit **KITTY**; through the back scene.

Enter **SAVILLE, FLUTTER**, and **MASKS**.

FLUTTER
O Gemini! beg the Petticoat's pardon.—Just saw a corner of it.

1st **MASK**
No wonder admittance was so difficult. I thought you took us for Bailiffs.

COURTALL
Upon my soul, I am devilish glad to see you—but you perceive how I am circumstanc'd. Excuse me at this moment.

2nd MASK
Tell us who 'tis then.

COURTALL
Oh, fie!

FLUTTER
We won't blab.

COURTALL

I can't, upon honour.—Thus far—She's a Woman of the first Character and Rank. Saville, [takes him aside] have I influence, or have I not?

SAVILLE
Why, sure, you do not insinuate—

COURTALL
No, not insinuate, but swear, that she's now in my bed-chamber:—by gad, I don't deceive you.—There's Generalship, you Rogue! Such an humble, distant, sighing Fellow as thou art, at the end of a six-months siege, would have boasted of a kiss from her glove.—I only give the signal, and—pop!—she's in my arms.

SAVILLE
What, Lady Fran—

COURTALL
Hush! You shall see her name to-morrow morning in red letters at the end of my list. Gentlemen, you must excuse me now. Come and drink chocolate at twelve, but—

SAVILLE
Aye, let us go, out of respect to the Lady:—'tis a Person of Rank.

FLUTTER
Is it?—Then I'll have a peep at her.

(Runs to the door in the back Scene.)

COURTALL
This is too much, Sir.

(Trying to prevent him.)

1st MASK
By Jupiter, we'll all have a peep.

COURTALL
Gentlemen, consider—for Heaven's sake—a Lady of Quality.
What will be the consequences?

FLUTTER
The consequences!—Why, you'll have your throat cut, that's all—but I'll write your Elegy. So, now for the door! [Part open the door, whilst the rest hold **COURTALL**.]—Beg your Ladyship's pardon, whoever you are: [Leads her out.] Emerge from darkness like the glorious Sun, and bless the wond'ring circle with your charms.

[Takes off her Mask.]

SAVILLE
Kitty Willis! ha! ha! ha!

OMNES
Kitty Willis! ha! ha! ha! Kitty Willis!

1st MASK
Why, what a Fellow you are, Courtall, to attempt imposing on your friends in this manner! A Lady of Quality—an Earl's Daughter—Your Ladyship's most obedient.—Ha! ha! ha!

SAVILLE
Courtall, have you influence, or have you not?

FLUTTER
The Man's moon-struck.

COURTALL
Hell, and ten thousand Furies, seize you all together!

KITTY
What! me, too, Mr. Courtall? me, whom you have knelt to, prayed to, and adored?

FLUTTER
That's right, Kitty; give him a little more.

COURTALL
Disappointed and laugh'd at!—

SAVILLE
Laugh'd at and despis'd. I have fullfilled my design, which was to expose your villainy, and laugh at your presumption. Adieu, Sir! Remember how you again boast of your influence with Women of Rank; and, when you next want amusement, dare not to look up to the virtuous and to the noble for a Companion.

[Exit, leading **KITTY**.

FLUTTER
And, Courtall, before you carry a Lady into your bed-chamber again, look under her mask, d'ye hear?

[Exit.

COURTALL
There's no bearing this! I'll set off for Paris directly.

[Exit.

ACT V

SCENE I.—Hardy's

Enter **MR HARDY** and **VILLERS**.

VILLERS
Whimsical enough! Dying for her, and hates her; believes her a Fool, and a Woman of brilliant Understanding!

MR HARDY
As true as you are alive;—but when I went up to him last night, at the Pantheon, out of downright good-nature to explain things—my Gentleman whips round upon his heel, and snapt me as short as if I had been a beggar-woman with six children, and he Overseer of the Parish.

VILLERS
Here comes the Wonder-worker—[Enter Letitia.] Here comes the Enchantress, who can go to Masquerades, and sing and dance, and talk a Man out of his wits!—But pray, have we Morning Masquerades?

LETITIA
Oh, no—but I am so enamour'd of this all-conquering Habit, that I could not resist putting it on, the moment I had breakfasted. I shall wear it on the day I am married, and then lay it by in spices—like the miraculous Robes of St. Bridget.

VILLERS
That's as most Brides do. The charms that helped to catch the Husband, are generally laid by, one after another, 'till the Lady grows a downright Wife, and then runs crying to her Mother, because she has transform'd her Lover into a downright Husband.

MR HARDY
Listen to me.—I ha'n't slept to-night, for thinking of plots to plague Doricourt;—and they drove one another out of my head so quick, that I was as giddy as a goose, and could make nothing of 'em.—I wish to goodness you could contrive something.

VILLERS
Contrive to plague him! Nothing so easy. Don't undeceive him, Madam, 'till he is your Husband. Marry him whilst he possesses the sentiments you labour'd to give him of Miss Hardy—and when you are his Wife—

LETITIA
Oh, Heavens! I see the whole—that's the very thing. My dear Mr. Villers, you are the divinest Man.

VILLERS
Don't make love to me, Hussey.

Enter **MRS RACKET**.

MRS RACKET

No, pray don't—for I design to have Villers myself in about six years.—There's an oddity in him that pleases me.—He holds Women in contempt; and I should like to have an opportunity of breaking his heart for that.

VILLERS
And when I am heartily tired of life, I know no Woman whom I would with more pleasure make my Executioner.

MR HARDY
It cannot be—I foresee it will be impossible to bring it about. You know the wedding wasn't to take place this week or more—and Letty will never be able to play the Fool so long.

VILLERS
The knot shall be tied to-night.—I have it all here, (pointing to his forehead:) the licence is ready. Feign yourself ill, send for Doricourt, and tell him you can't go out of the world in peace, except you see the ceremony performed.

MR HARDY
I feign myself ill! I could as soon feign myself a Roman Ambassador.—I was never ill in my life, but with the tooth-ach—when Letty's Mother was a breeding I had all the qualms.

VILLERS
Oh, I have no fears for you.—But what says Miss Hardy? Are you willing to make the irrevocable vow before night?

LETITIA
Oh, Heavens!—I—I—'Tis so exceeding sudden, that really—

MRS RACKET
That really she is frighten'd out of her wits—lest it should be impossible to bring matters about. But I have taken the scheme into my protection, and you shall be Mrs. Doricourt before night. Come, [to **MR HARDY**] to bed directly: your room shall be cramm'd with phials, and all the apparatus of Death;—then heigh presto! For Doricourt.

VILLERS
You go and put off your conquering dress, [to **LETITIA**] and get all your aukward airs ready—And you practise a few groans [to **MR HARDY**.]—And you—if possible—an air of gravity [to **MRS RACKET**]. I'll answer for the plot.

LETITIA
Married in jest! 'Tis an odd idea! Well, I'll venture it.

[Exit **LETITIA** and **MRS RACKET**.

VILLERS
Aye, I'll be sworn! [looks at his watch] 'tis past three. The Budget's to be open'd this morning. I'll just step down to the House.—Will you go?

MR HARDY
What! with a mortal sickness?

VILLERS
What a Blockhead! I believe, if half of us were to stay away with mortal sicknesses, it would be for the health of the Nation. Good-morning.—I'll call and feel your pulse as I come back.

[Exit.

MR HARDY
You won't find 'em over brisk, I fancy. I foresee some ill happening from this making believe to die before one's time. But hang it—a-hem!—I am a stout man yet; only fifty-six—What's that? In the last Yearly Bill there were three lived to above an hundred. Fifty-six!—Fiddle-de-dee! I am not afraid, not I.

[Exit.

SCENE II.—Doricourt's

DORICOURT in his Robe-de-Chambre.

Enter **SAVILLE**.

SAVILLE
Undress'd so late?

DORICOURT
I didn't go to bed 'till late—'twas late before I slept—late when I rose. Do you know Lord George Jennett?

SAVILLE
Yes.

DORICOURT
Has he a Mistress?

SAVILLE
Yes.

DORICOURT
What sort of a creature is she?

SAVILLE
Why, she spends him three thousand a year with the ease of a Duchess, and entertains his friends with the grace of a Ninon. Ergo, she is handsome, spirited, and clever.

[**DORICOURT** walks about disordered.]

In the name of Caprice, what ails you?

DORICOURT
You have hit it—Elle est mon Caprice—The Mistress of Lord George Jennett is my caprice—Oh, insufferable!

SAVILLE
What, you saw her at the Masquerade?

DORICOURT
Saw her, lov'd her, died for her—without knowing her—And now the curse is, I can't hate her.

SAVILLE
Ridiculous enough! All this distress about a Kept Woman, whom any man may have, I dare swear, in a fortnight—They've been jarring some time.

DORICOURT
Have her! The sentiment I have conceived for the Witch is so unaccountable, that, in that line, I cannot bear her idea. Was she a Woman of Honour, for a Wife, I cou'd adore her—but, I really believe, if she should send me an assignation, I should hate her.

SAVILLE
Hey-day! This sounds like Love. What becomes of poor Miss Hardy?

DORICOURT
Her name has given me an ague. Dear Saville, how shall I contrive to make old Hardy cancel the engagements! The moiety of the estate which he will forfeit, shall be his the next moment, by deed of gift.

SAVILLE
Let me see—Can't you get it insinuated that you are a dev'lish wild fellow; that you are an Infidel, and attached to wenching, gaming, and so forth?

DORICOURT
Aye, such a character might have done some good two centuries back.—But who the devil can it frighten now? I believe it must be the mad scheme, at last.—There, will that do for the grin?

SAVILLE
Ridiculous!—But, how are you certain that the Woman who has so bewildered you, belongs to Lord George?

DORICOURT
Flutter told me so.

SAVILLE
Then fifty to one against the intelligence.

DORICOURT

It must be so. There was a mystery in her manner, for which nothing else can account. [A violent rap.] Who can this be?

[**SAVILLE** looks out.]

SAVILLE

The proverb is your answer—'tis Flutter himself. Tip him a scene of the Mad-man, and see how it takes.

DORICOURT

I will—a good way to send it about town. Shall it be of the melancholy kind, or the raving?

SAVILLE

Rant!—rant!—Here he comes.

DORICOURT

Talk not to me who can pull comets by the beard, and overset an island!

Enter **FLUTTER**.

There! This is he!—this is he who hath sent my poor soul, without coat or breeches, to be tossed about in ether like a duck-feather! Villain, give me my soul again!

FLUTTER

Upon my soul I hav'n't got it. [Exceedingly frightened.]

SAVILLE

Oh, Mr. Flutter, what a melancholy sight!—I little thought to have seen my poor friend reduced to this.

FLUTTER

Mercy defend me! What's he mad?

SAVILLE

You see how it is. A cursed Italian Lady—Jealousy—gave him a drug; and every full of the moon—

DORICOURT

Moon! Who dares talk of the Moon? The patroness of genius—the rectifier of wits—the—Oh! here she is!—I feel her—she tugs at my brain—she has it—she has it—Oh!

[Exit.

FLUTTER

Well! this is dreadful! exceeding dreadful, I protest. Have you had Monro?

SAVILLE

Not yet. The worthy Miss Hardy—what a misfortune!

FLUTTER

Aye, very true.—Do they know it?

SAVILLE
Oh, no; the paroxysm seized him but this morning.

FLUTTER
Adieu! I can't stay.

[Going in great haste.]

SAVILLE
But you must. (holding him) Stay, and assist me:—perhaps he'll return again in a moment; and, when he is in this way, his strength is prodigious.

FLUTTER
Can't indeed—can't upon my soul.

[Exit.

SAVILLE
Flutter—Don't make a mistake, now;—remember 'tis Doricourt that's mad.

[Exit.

FLUTTER
Yes—you mad.

SAVILLE
No, no; Doricourt.

FLUTTER
Egad, I'll say you are both mad, and then I can't mistake.

[Exeunt severally.

SCENE III.—Sir George Touchwood's

Enter **SIR GEORGE**, and **LADY FRANCES**.

SIR GEORGE
The bird is escaped—Courtall is gone to France.

LADY FRANCES
Heaven and earth! Have ye been to seek him?

SIR GEORGE

Seek him! Aye.

LADY FRANCES
How did you get his name? I should never have told it you.

SIR GEORGE
I learnt it in the first Coffee-house I entered.—Every body is full of the story.

LADY FRANCES
Thank Heaven! he's gone!—But I have a story for you—The Hardy family are forming a plot upon your Friend Doricourt, and we are expected in the evening to assist.

SIR GEORGE
With all my heart, my Angel; but I can't stay to hear it unfolded. They told me Mr. Saville would be at home in half an hour, and I am impatient to see him. The adventure of last night—

LADY FRANCES
Think of it only with gratitude. The danger I was in has overset a new system of conduct, that, perhaps, I was too much inclined to adopt. But henceforward, my dear Sir George, you shall be my constant Companion, and Protector. And, when they ridicule the unfashionable Monsters, the felicity of our hearts shall make their satire pointless.

SIR GEORGE
Charming Angel! You almost reconcile me to Courtall. Hark! here's company (stepping to the door.) 'Tis your lively Widow—I'll step down the back stairs, to escape her.

[Exit Sir George.

Enter **MRS RACKET**.

MRS RACKET
Oh, Lady Frances! I am shock'd to death.—Have you received
a card from us?

LADY FRANCES
Yes; within these twenty minutes.

MRS RACKET
Aye, 'tis of no consequence.—'Tis all over—Doricourt is mad.

LADY FRANCES
Mad!

MRS RACKET
My poor Letitia!—Just as we were enjoying ourselves with the prospect of a scheme that was planned for their mutual happiness, in came Flutter, breathless, with the intelligence:—I flew here to know if you had heard it.

LADY FRANCES

No, indeed—and I hope it is one of Mr. Flutter's dreams.

Enter **SAVILLE**.

A-propos; now we shall be informed. Mr. Saville, I rejoice to see you, though Sir George will be disappointed: he's gone to your lodgings.

SAVILLE

I should have been happy to have prevented Sir George. I hope your Ladyship's adventure last night did not disturb your dreams?

LADY FRANCES

Not at all; for I never slept a moment. My escape, and the importance of my obligations to you, employed my thoughts. But we have just had shocking intelligence—Is it true that Doricourt is mad?

SAVILLE

So; the business is done. (Aside.) Madam, I am sorry to say, that I have just been a melancholy witness of his ravings: he was in the height of a paroxysm.

MRS RACKET

Oh, there can be no doubt of it. Flutter told us the whole history. Some Italian Princess gave him a drug, in a box of sweetmeats, sent to him by her own page; and it renders him lunatic every month. Poor Miss Hardy! I never felt so much on any occasion in my life.

SAVILLE

To soften your concern, I will inform you, Madam, that Miss Hardy is less to be pitied than you imagine.

MRS RACKET

Why so, Sir?

SAVILLE

'Tis rather a delicate subject—but he did not love Miss Hardy.

MRS RACKET

He did love Miss Hardy, Sir, and would have been the happiest of men.

SAVILLE

Pardon me, Madam; his heart was not only free from that Lady's chains, but absolutely captivated by another.

MRS RACKET

No, Sir—no. It was Miss Hardy who captivated him. She met him last night at the Masquerade, and charmed him in disguise—He professed the most violent passion for her; and a plan was laid, this evening, to cheat him into happiness.

SAVILLE

Ha! ha! ha!—Upon my soul, I must beg your pardon; I have not eaten of the Italian Princess's box of sweetmeats, sent by her own page; and yet I am as mad as Doricourt, ha! ha! ha!

MRS RACKET
So it appears—What can all this mean?

SAVILLE
Why, Madam, he is at present in his perfect senses; but he'll lose 'em in ten minutes, through joy.—The madness was only a feint, to avoid marrying Miss Hardy, ha! ha! ha!—I'll carry him the intelligence directly.

(Going.)

MRS RACKET
Not for worlds. I owe him revenge, now, for what he has made us suffer. You must promise not to divulge a syllable I have told you; and when Doricourt is summoned to Mr. Hardy's, prevail on him to come—madness, and all.

LADY FRANCES
Pray do. I should like to see him shewing off, now I am in the secret.

SAVILLE
You must be obeyed; though 'tis inhuman to conceal his happiness.

MRS RACKET
I am going home; so I'll set you down at his lodgings, and acquaint you, by the way, with our whole scheme. Allons!

SAVILLE
I attend you

(leading her out.)

MRS RACKET
You won't fail us?

[Exit **SAVILLE**, and **MRS RACKET**.

LADY FRANCES
No; depend on us.

[Exit.

SCENE IV.—Doricourt's

DORICOURT seated, reading.

DORICOURT (flings away the book)

What effect can the morals of Fourscore have on a mind torn with passion? (musing) Is it possible such a soul as her's, can support itself in so humiliating a situation? A kept Woman! (rising) Well, well—I am glad it is so—I am glad it is so!

Enter **SAVILLE**.

SAVILLE

What a happy dog you are, Doricourt! I might have been mad, or beggar'd, or pistol'd myself, without its being mentioned—But you, forsooth! the whole Female World is concerned for. I reported the state of your brain to five different women—The lip of the first trembled; the white bosom of the second heaved a sigh; the third ejaculated, and turned her eye—to the glass; the fourth blessed herself; and the fifth said, whilst she pinned a curl, "Well, now, perhaps, he'll be an amusing Companion; his native dullness was intolerable."

DORICOURT

Envy! sheer envy, by the smiles of Hebe!—There are not less than forty pair of the brightest eyes in town will drop crystals, when they hear of my misfortune.

SAVILLE

Well, but I have news for you:—Poor Hardy is confined to his bed; they say he is going out of the world by the first post, and he wants to give you his blessing.

DORICOURT

Ill! so ill! I am sorry from my soul. He's a worthy little Fellow—if he had not the gift of foreseeing so strongly.

SAVILLE

Well; you must go and take leave.

DORICOURT

What! to act the Lunatic in the dying Man's chamber?

SAVILLE

Exactly the thing; and will bring your business to a short issue: for his last commands must be, That you are not to marry his Daughter.

DORICOURT

That's true, by Jupiter!—and yet, hang it, impose upon a poor fellow at so serious a moment!—I can't do it.

SAVILLE

You must, 'faith. I am answerable for your appearance, though it should be in a strait waistcoat. He knows your situation, and seems the more desirous of an interview.

DORICOURT

I don't like encountering Racket.—She's an arch little devil, and will discover the cheat.

SAVILLE
There's a fellow!—Cheated Ninety-nine Women, and now afraid of the Hundredth.

DORICOURT
And with reason—for that hundredth is a Widow.

[Exeunt.

SCENE V.—Hardy's

Enter **MRS RACKET**, and **MISS OGLE**.

MISS OGLE
And so Miss Hardy is actually to be married to-night?

MRS RACKET
If her Fate does not deceive her. You are apprised of the scheme, and we hope it will succeed.

MISS OGLE
Deuce, take her! she's six years younger than I am. (Aside)—Is Mr. Doricourt handsome?

MRS RACKET
Handsome, generous, young, and rich.—There's a Husband for ye! Isn't he worth pulling caps for?

MISS OGLE
I' my conscience, the Widow speaks as though she'd give cap, ears, and all for him. (Aside.) I wonder you didn't try to catch this wonderful Man, Mrs. Racket?

MRS RACKET
Really, Miss Ogle, I had not time. Besides, when I marry, so many stout young fellows will hang themselves, that, out of regard to society, in these sad times, I shall postpone it for a few years. This will cost her a new lace—I heard it crack. (Aside.)

Enter **SIR GEORGE**, and **LADY FRANCES**.

SIR GEORGE
Well, here we are.—But where's the Knight of the Woeful Countenance?

MRS RACKET
Here soon, I hope—for a woeful Night it will be without him.

SIR GEORGE
Oh, fie! do you condescend to pun?

MRS RACKET

Why not? It requires genius to make a good pun—some men of bright parts can't reach it. I know a Lawyer who writes them on the back of his briefs; and says they are of great use—in a dry cause.

Enter **FLUTTER**.

FLUTTER
Here they come!—Here they come!—Their coach stopped, as mine drove off.

LADY FRANCES
Then Miss Hardy's fate is at a crisis.—She plays a hazardous game, and I tremble for her.

SAVILLE (without)
Come, let me guide you!—This way, my poor Friend!
Why are you so furious?

DORICOURT (without)
The House of Death—to the House of Death!

Enter **DORICOURT**, and **SAVILLE**.

Ah! this is the spot!

LADY FRANCES
How wild and fiery he looks!

MISS OGLE
Now, I think, he looks terrified.

FLUTTER
Poor creature, how his eyes work!

MRS RACKET
I never saw a Madman before—Let me examine him—Will he bite?

SAVILLE
Pray keep out of his reach, Ladies—You don't know your danger.
He's like a Wild Cat, if a sudden thought seises him.

SIR GEORGE
You talk like a Keeper of Wild Cats—How much do you demand for shewing the Monster?

DORICOURT
I don't like this—I must rouse their sensibility. There! there she darts through the air in liquid flames! Down again! Now I have her—Oh, she burns, she scorches!—Oh! she eats into my very heart!

OMNES
Ha! ha! ha!

MRS RACKET
He sees the Apparition of the wicked Italian Princess.

FLUTTER
Keep her Highness fast, Doricourt.

MISS OGLE
Give her a pinch, before you let her go.

DORICOURT
I am laughed at!

MRS RACKET
Laughed at—aye, to be sure; why, I could play the Madman better than you.—There! there she is! Now I have her! Ha! ha! ha!

DORICOURT
I knew that Devil would discover me. (Aside) I'll leave the house:—I'm covered with confusion.

(Going.)

SIR GEORGE
Stay, Sir—You must not go. 'Twas poorly done, Mr. Doricourt, to affect madness, rather than fulfil your engagements.

DORICOURT
Affect madness!—Saville, what can I do?

SAVILLE
Since you are discovered, confess the whole.

MISS OGLE
Aye, turn Evidence, and save Yourself.

DORICOURT
Yes; since my designs have been so unaccountably discovered, I will avow the whole. I cannot love Miss Hardy—and I will never—

SAVILLE
Hold, my dear Doricourt! be not so rash. What will the world say to such—

DORICOURT
Damn the world! What will the world give me for the loss of happiness? Must I sacrifice my peace, to please the world?

SIR GEORGE
Yes, every thing, rather than be branded with dishonour.

LADY FRANCES

Though our arguments should fail, there is a Pleader, whom you surely cannot withstand—the dying Mr. Hardy supplicates you not to forsake his Child.

Enter **VILLERS**.

VILLERS

Mr. Hardy requests you to grant him a moment's conversation, Mr. Doricourt, though you should persist to send him miserable to the grave. Let me conduct you to his chamber.

DORICOURT

Oh, aye, any where; to the Antipodes—to the Moon—Carry me—Do with me what you will.

MRS RACKET

Mortification and disappointment, then, are specifics in a case of stubbornness.—I'll follow, and let you know what passes.

[Exeunt **VILLERS**, **DORICOURT**, **MRS RACKET**, and **MISS OGLE**.

FLUTTER

Ladies, Ladies, have the charity to take me with you, that I may make no blunder in repeating the story.

[Exit **FLUTTER**.

LADY FRANCES

Sir George, you don't know Mr. Saville.

[Exit **LADY FRANCES**.

SIR GEORGE

Ten thousand pardons—but I will not pardon myself, for not observing you. I have been with the utmost impatience at your door twice to-day.

SAVILLE

I am concerned you had so much trouble, Sir George.

SIR GEORGE

Trouble! what a word!—I hardly know how to address you; I am distressed beyond measure; and it is the highest proof of my opinion of your honour, and the delicacy of your mind, that I open my heart to you.

SAVILLE

What has disturbed you, Sir George?

SIR GEORGE

Your having preserved Lady Frances, in so imminent a danger. Start not, Saville; to protect Lady Frances, was my right. You have wrested from me my dearest privilege.

SAVILLE

I hardly know how to answer such a reproach. I cannot apologize for what I have done.

SIR GEORGE

I do not mean to reproach you; I hardly know what I mean. There is one method by which you may restore peace to me; I cannot endure that my Wife should be so infinitely indebted to any man who is less than my Brother.

SAVILLE

Pray explain yourself.

SIR GEORGE

I have a Sister, Saville, who is amiable; and you are worthy of her. I shall give her a commission to steal your heart, out of revenge for what you have done.

SAVILLE

I am infinitely honoured, Sir George; but—

SIR GEORGE

I cannot listen to a sentence which begins with so unpromising a word. You must go with us into Hampshire; and, if you see each other with the eyes I do, your felicity will be complete. I know no one, to whose heart I would so readily commit the care of my Sister's happiness.

SAVILLE

I will attend you to Hampshire, with pleasure; but not on the plan of retirement. Society has claims on Lady Frances, that forbid it.

SIR GEORGE

Claims, Saville!

SAVILLE

Yes, claims; Lady Frances was born to be the ornament of Courts. She is sufficiently alarmed, not to wander beyond the reach of her Protector;—and, from the British Court, the most tenderly-anxious Husband could not wish to banish his Wife. Bid her keep in her eye the bright Example who presides there; the splendour of whose rank yields to the superior lustre of her Virtue.

SIR GEORGE

I allow the force of your argument. Now for intelligence!

Enter **MRS RACKET**, **LADY FRANCES**, and **FLUTTER**.

MRS RACKET

Oh! Heav'ns! do you know—

FLUTTER

Let me tell the story—As soon as Doricourt—

MRS RACKET

I protest you sha'n't—said Mr. Hardy—

FLUTTER
No, 'twas Doricourt spoke first—says he—No, 'twas the Parson—says he—

MRS RACKET
Stop his mouth, Sir George—he'll spoil the tale.

SIR GEORGE
Never heed circumstances—the result—the result.

MRS RACKET
No, no; you shall have it in form.—Mr. Hardy performed the Sick Man like an Angel—He sat up in his bed, and talked so pathetically, that the tears stood in Doricourt's eyes.

FLUTTER
Aye, stood—they did not drop, but stood.—I shall, in future, be very exact. The Parson seized the moment; you know, they never miss an opportunity.

MRS RACKET
Make haste, said Doricourt; if I have time to reflect, poor Hardy will die unhappy.

FLUTTER
They were got as far as the Day of Judgement, when we slipt out of the room.

SIR GEORGE
Then, by this time, they must have reached Amazement, which, every body knows, is the end of Matrimony.

MRS RACKET
Aye, the Reverend Fathers ended the service with that word, Prophetically—to teach the Bride what a capricious Monster a Husband is.

SIR GEORGE
I rather think it was Sarcastically—to prepare the Bridegroom for the unreasonable humours and vagaries of his Help-mate.

LADY FRANCES
Here comes the Bridegroom of to-night.

Enter **DORICOURT** and **VILLERS**.—**VILLERS** whispers to **SAVILLE**, who goes out.

OMNES
Joy! joy! joy!

MISS OGLE
If he's a sample of Bridegrooms, keep me single!—A younger Brother, from the Funeral of his Father, could not carry a more fretful countenance.

FLUTTER

Oh!—Now, he's melancholy mad, I suppose.

LADY FRANCES

You do not consider the importance of the occasion.

VILLERS

No; nor how shocking a thing it is for a Man to be forced to marry one Woman, whilst his heart is devoted to another.

MRS RACKET

Well, now 'tis over, I confess to you, Mr. Doricourt, I think 'twas a most ridiculous piece of Quixotism, to give up the happiness of a whole life to a Man who perhaps has but a few moments to be sensible of the sacrifice.

FLUTTER

So it appeared to me.—But, thought I, Mr. Doricourt has travelled—he knows best.

DORICOURT

Zounds! Confusion!—Did ye not all set upon me?—Didn't ye talk to me of Honour—Compassion—Justice?

SIR GEORGE

Very true—You have acted according to their dictates, and I hope the utmost felicity of the Married State will reward you.

DORICOURT

Never, Sir George! To Felicity I bid adieu—but I will endeavour to be content. Where is my—I must speak it—where is my Wife?

Enter **LETITIA**, masked, led by **SAVILLE**.

SAVILLE

Mr. Doricourt, this Lady was pressing to be introduced to you.

DORICOURT

Oh! (Starting).

LETITIA

I told you last night, you shou'd see me at a time when you least expected me—and I have kept my promise.

VILLERS

Whoever you are, Madam, you could not have arrived at a happier moment.—Mr. Doricourt is just married.

LETITIA

Married! Impossible! 'Tis but a few hours since he swore to me eternal Love: I believ'd him, gave him up my Virgin heart—and now!—Ungrateful Sex!

DORICOURT
Your Virgin heart! No, Lady—my fate, thank Heaven! yet wants that torture. Nothing but the conviction that you was another's, could have made me think one moment of Marriage, to have saved the lives of half Mankind. But this visit, Madam, is as barbarous as unexpected. It is now my duty to forget you, which, spite of your situation, I found difficult enough.

LETITIA
My situation!—What situation?

DORICOURT
I must apologise for explaining it in this company—but, Madam, I am not ignorant, that you are the companion of Lord George Jennet—and this is the only circumstance that can give me peace.

LETITIA
I—a Companion! Ridiculous pretence! No, Sir, know, to your confusion, that my heart, my honour, my name is unspotted as her's you have married; my birth equal to your own, my fortune large—That, and my person, might have been your's.—But, Sir, farewell!

(Going.)

DORICOURT
Oh, stay a moment—Rascal! is she not—

FLUTTER
Who, she? O Lard! no—'Twas quite a different person that I meant.—I never saw that Lady before.

DORICOURT
Then, never shalt thou see her more.

[Shakes **FLUTTER**.]

MRS RACKET
Have mercy upon the poor Man!—Heavens! He'll murder him.

DORICOURT
Murder him! Yes, you, myself, and all Mankind. Sir George—Saville—Villers—'twas you who push'd me on this precipice;—'tis you who have snatch'd from me joy, felicity, and life.

MRS RACKET
There! Now, how well he acts the Madman!—This is something like! I knew he would do it well enough, when the time came.

DORICOURT
Hard-hearted Woman! enjoy my ruin—riot in my wretchedness.

[**MR HARDY** bursts in.]

MR HARDY
This is too much. You are now the Husband of my Daughter; and how dare you shew all this passion about another Woman?

DORICOURT
Alive again!

MR HARDY
Alive! aye, and merry. Here, wipe off the flour from my face. I was never in better health and spirits in my life.—I foresaw t'would do—. Why, my illness was only a fetch, Man! to make you marry Letty.

DORICOURT
It was! Base and ungenerous! Well, Sir, you shall be gratified. The possession of my heart was no object either with You, or your Daughter. My fortune and name was all you desired, and these—I leave ye. My native England I shall quit, nor ever behold you more. But, Lady, that in my exile I may have one consolation, grant me the favour you denied last night;—let me behold all that mask conceals, that your whole image may be impress'd on my heart, and chear my distant solitary hours.

LETITIA
This is the most awful moment of my life. Oh, Doricourt, the slight action of taking off my Mask, stamps me the most blest or miserable of Women!

DORICOURT
What can this mean? Reveal your face, I conjure you.

LETITIA
Behold it.

DORICOURT
Rapture! Transport! Heaven!

FLUTTER
Now for a touch of the happy Madman.

VILLERS
This scheme was mine.

LETITIA
I will not allow that. This little stratagem arose from my disappointment, in not having made the impression on you I wish'd. The timidity of the English character threw a veil over me, you could not penetrate. You have forced me to emerge in some measure from my natural reserve, and to throw off the veil that hid me.

DORICOURT
I am yet in a state of intoxication—I cannot answer you.—Speak on, sweet Angel!

LETITIA

You see I can be any thing; chuse then my character—your Taste shall fix it. Shall I be an English Wife?—or, breaking from the bonds of Nature and Education, step forth to the world in all the captivating glare of Foreign Manners?

DORICOURT

You shall be nothing but yourself—nothing can be captivating that you are not. I will not wrong your penetration, by pretending that you won my heart at the first interview; but you have now my whole soul—your person, your face, your mind, I would not exchange for those of any other Woman breathing.

MR HARDY

A Dog! how well he makes up for past slights! Cousin Racket, I wish you a good Husband with all my heart. Mr. Flutter, I'll believe every word you say this fortnight. Mr. Villers, you and I have manag'd this to a T. I never was so merry in my life—'Gad, I believe I can dance. (Footing.)

DORICOURT

Charming, charming creature!

LETITIA

Congratulate me, my dear friends! Can you conceive my happiness?

MR HARDY

No, congratulate me; for mine is the greatest.

FLUTTER

No, congratulate me, that I have escaped with life, and give me some sticking plaster—this wild cat has torn the skin from my throat.

SIR GEORGE

I expect to be among the first who are congratulated—for I have recovered one Angel, while Doricourt has gained another.

MR HARDY

Pho! pho! Don't talk of Angels, we shall be happier by half as Mortals. Come into the next room; I have order'd out every drop of my Forty-eight, and I'll invite the whole parish of St. George's, but what we'll drink it out—except one dozen, which I shall keep under three double locks, for a certain Christening, that I foresee will happen within this twelvemonth.

DORICOURT

My charming Bride! It was a strange perversion of Taste, that led me to consider the delicate timidity of your deportment, as the mark of an uninform'd mind, or inelegant manners. I feel now it is to that innate modesty, English Husbands owe a felicity the Married Men of other nations are strangers to: it is a sacred veil to your own charms; it is the surest bulwark to your Husband's honour; and cursed be the hour—should it ever arrive—in which British Ladies shall sacrifice to foreign Graces the Grace of Modesty!

FINIS.

EPILOGUE

Nay, cease, and hear me—I am come to scold—
Whence this night's plaudits, to a thought so old?
To gain a Lover, hid behind a Mask!
What's new in that? or where's the mighty task?
For instance, now—What Lady Bab, or Grace,
E'er won a Lover—in her natural Face?
Mistake me not—French red, or blanching creams,
I stoop not to—for those are hackney'd themes;
The arts I mean, are harder to detect,
Easier put on, and worn to more effect;—
As thus—
Do Pride and Envy, with their horrid lines,
Destroy th' effect of Nature's sweet designs?
The Mask of Softness is at once applied,
And gentlest manners ornament the Bride.
Do thoughts too free inform the Vestal's eye,
Or point the glance, or warm the struggling sigh?
Not Dian's brows more rigid looks disclose;
And Virtue's blush appears, where Passion glows.

And you, my gentle Sirs, wear Vizors too;
But here I'll strip you, and expose to view
Your hidden features—First I point at you.
That well-stuff'd waistcoat, and that ruddy cheek;
That ample forehead, and that skin so sleek,
Point out good-nature, and a gen'rous heart—
Tyrant! stand forth, and, conscious, own thy part:
Thy Wife, thy Children, tremble in thy eye;
And Peace is banish'd—when the Father's nigh.

Sure 'tis enchantment! See, from ev'ry side
The Masks fall off!—In charity I hide
The monstrous features rushing to my view—
Fear not, there, Grand-Papa—nor you—nor you:
For should I shew your features to each other,
Not one amongst ye'd know his Friend, or Brother.
'Tis plain, then, all the world, from Youth to Age,
Appear in Masks—Here, only, on the Stage,
You see us as we are: Here trust your eyes;
Our wish to please, admits of no disguise.

Hannah Cowley – A Short Biography

Hannah Cowley was born Hannah Parkhouse on March 14th, 1743, the daughter of Hannah (née Richards) and Philip Parkhouse, a bookseller in Tiverton, Devon.

As one might expect details of much of her life are scant and that of her early life almost non-existent.

However, we do know that she married Thomas Cowley in either 1768 or 1772 and that the marriage produced 3 or perhaps 4 children.

The couple moved to London after their marriage and Thomas worked as an official in the Stamp Office and as a part-time journalist.

Her career in the literary world seemed to happen rather late. It was whilst the couple were attending a play, thought to be sometime in late 1775, that Cowley was struck by a sudden necessity to write. "So delighted with this?" she boasted to him. "Why I could write as well myself!"

And she set to work. By the next day she showed him the first act of her comedy; The Runaway. She set about finishing the rest of the play and then sent it to the famed actor-manager, David Garrick. It was produced at his final season at the Drury Lane theatre on February 15th, 1776.

The Runaway enjoyed 17 performances in its first season at Drury Lane and was revived many times thereafter.

Its initial success, and the encouragement of the newly retired Garrick, ensured that Cowley would write more. She wrote her next two plays, the farce, Who's the Dupe? and the tragedy, Albina, before the year was out.

Who's the Dupe? and Albina encountered several difficulties getting into production. The new manager of Drury Lane, Richard Brinsley Sheridan, postponed The Runaway for most of the 1777 season. Upset, Cowley thought of an alternate means to get her play produced. She sent Albina to Drury Lane's rival theatre in London, Covent Garden. Alas it was not accepted. Albina now bounced back and forth between the two theatres for the next two years. Meanwhile, Sheridan agreed to produce Who's the Dupe? but the premiere would only take place in the spring, an unprofitable time for a new play to open.

The play brought controversy. Her rival Hannah More had written Percy and it opened in 1777. Cowley thought several parts of it were similar to her own, as yet, un-produced play. It raised her suspicions. When Hannah More next had The Fatal Falsehood open in 1779 Cowley was convinced that More had plagarised from her own Albina.

Indeed when The Fatal Falsehood opened on May 6th, 1779, it was followed by charges in the press that More stole her ideas from Cowley. On August 10th, More wrote to the St. James Chronicle to protest that she "never saw, heard, or read, a single line of Mrs. Cowley's Tragedy." Cowley herself was hurt but acted with good grace. She wrote in a later printed preface to Albina that hers and More's plays do indeed have "wonderful resemblances." And she allowed that theatre managers, who in those days also acted as script editors, may have inadvertently given More her ideas: "Amidst the crowd of Plots, and Stage Contrivances, in which a Manager is involv'd, recollection is too frequently mistaken for the suggestions of imagination"

Albina finally opened on July 31st, 1779, at the Haymarket to neither financial nor critical success.

With the Hannah More controversy behind her, Cowley wrote her most popular comedy, The Belle's Stratagem. It was staged at Covent Garden in 1780. In its first season it performed for 28 nights and was regularly revived helping to ensure a solid revenue stream for Cowley and her family.

Her next play, The World as It Goes; or, a Party at Montpelier (the title was later changed to Second Thoughts Are Best) was unsuccessful, but she continued to write and there followed another seven plays; Which is the Man?; A Bold Stroke for a Husband; More Ways Than One; A School for Greybeards, or, The Mourning Bride; The Fate of Sparta, or, The Rival Kings; A Day in Turkey, or, The Russian Slaves and The Town Before You.

Sadly, none could recreate her initial triumph.

In 1783, Thomas Cowley accepted a job with the British East India Company and left for India leaving his wife in London to continue her career and to raise their children. Thomas never returned to England and died in India in 1797.

As well as plays Cowley also wrote poetry. In 1786, she wrote "The Scottish Village, or Pitcairne Green".

In 1787, under pseudonym "Anna Matilda," she and the poet Robert Merry (under his own pseudonym of "Della Crusca") began a poetic correspondence through the pages of The World journal. The poems were sentimental and flirtatious. Initially they did not even know the others' identity; but they later met and became part the Della Cruscans poetry movement. This volume of poetry was published under her pseudonym in 1788 as The Poetry of Anna Matilda.

Cowley's last play, The Town Before You, was produced in 1795.

In 1801 Cowley published perhaps her greatest poetical work. A six-book epic "The Siege of Acre: An Epic Poem".

That same year Cowley retired to Tiverton in Devon, where she spent her remaining years out of the public spotlight whilst she quietly revised her plays.

In her day, Cowley's works were popular and thought provoking. One critic noted she was "one of the foremost playwrights of the late eighteenth century" whose "skill in writing fluid, sparkling dialogue and creating sprightly, memorable comic characters compares favourably with her better-known contemporaries, Goldsmith and Sheridan."

Hannah Cowley died of liver failure on March 11th, 1809.

Hannah Cowley – A Concise Bibliography

Plays
The Runaway (1775, Staged 1776)

Who's the Dupe? (1776, Staged 1779)
Albina (1776, Staged 1779)
The Belle's Stratagem (1780)
The World as It Goes; or, a Party at Montpelier
Which is the Man?
A Bold Stroke for a Husband (1783)
More Ways Than One
A School for Greybeards, or, The Mourning Bride
The Fate of Sparta, or, The Rival Kings
A Day in Turkey, or, The Russian Slaves
The Town Before You (1795)

Poetry

The Scottish Village, or Pitcairne Green (1786)
The Poetry of Anna Matilda (A pseudonym) includes A Tale for Jealousy and The Funeral (1788)
The Siege of Acre: an Epic Poem (1801)

Scenarios of Some of Her Plays

The Runaway (1776)

George Hargrave, who is home from college, is overjoyed to learn that Emily, the mysterious runaway whom his godfather, Mr. Drummond, has taken in, is the same young lady he fell in love with at a recent masquerade. Meanwhile, George's spirited cousin, Bella, helps George's sister, Harriet, and George's friend Sir Charles fall in love. George's designs are threatened when he learns that his father wants George to marry Lady Dinah, a pretentious older lady who is also very rich. When Emily's father arrives to take Emily back to London, George gives chase and snatches Emily back. Mr. Drummond saves the day by offering the young lovers some of his land so that they can have a fortune of their own.

Who's the Dupe? (1779)

Granger, a captain, arrives in town to see his lover, Elizabeth. Her uneducated father, Abraham Doiley, has promised her hand to the most educated man he can find, an unappealing but intelligent scholar named Gradus. Elizabeth's friend Charlotte, who fancies Gradus for herself, persuades Gradus to act more fashionable and less bookish so that he can win Elizabeth's heart. Doiley is not impressed by the new Gradus; meanwhile, Granger presents himself to Doiley as a scholar so that he can win Elizabeth's hand. Granger and Gradus square off against each other to see who is the more educated, and Granger wins by using phony Greek that nonetheless impresses Doiley. Gradus is consoled by winning Charlotte.

Albina (1779)

The powerful Duke of Westmorland learns that the gallant young soldier Edward is in love with his daughter, Albina, who is a young widow to Count Raimond. Despite her love for Edward, Albina's virtue impedes her from agreeing to marry him. Westmorland and Edward persuade her to remarry because Edward is soon destined to go off to war; she agrees. Editha, who is jealous of Albina, seeks help from Lord Gondibert, Raimond's brother, who secretly loves Albina. On the eve of the wedding, Gondibert tells Edward that Albina has been unfaithful, and to prove it he disguises himself and allows Edward to spy on him sneaking into Albina's chamber at night. Edward then calls off the wedding, and the furious

Westmorland challenges him to a duel to protect Albina's honour. Before the duel begins, Gondibert's elderly servant, Egbert, exposes his master's lie, and the king banishes Gondibert. Before he leaves, Gondibert vows to kill Albina and then commit suicide. He sneaks into Albina's chamber and stabs a woman he thinks is Albina, and then he stabs himself. But the woman turns out to be a disguised Editha, who had also stolen into the room. Edward is relieved when the real Albina rushes into the room, and the dying Gondibert asks for and receives her pardon.

The Belle's Stratagem (1780)
Having returned from his trip to Europe, the handsome Doricourt meets his betrothed, Letitia. He finds her acceptable but by no means as elegant as European women. Determined that she will not marry without love, Letitia enlists the help of her father, Mr. Hardy, and Mrs. Racket, a widow, to turn Doricourt off the wedding by pretending that she, Letitia, is an unmannerly hoyden. Meanwhile, Doricourt's friend Sir George is being overprotective of his new wife, Lady Frances, who rebels and agrees to accompany Mrs. Racket for a day in the town and a masquerade ball that night. While out at an auction, Lady Frances meets the rake, Courtall, who brags to his friend Saville that he will seduce her. Meanwhile, Letitia's brazen acting succeeds in dissuading Doricourt from wanting to marry her. All characters converge at that night's masquerade. The disguised Letitia shows off her charms, bewitches Doricourt and then leaves before he can find out who she is. Courtall, disguised the same way as Sir George, lures the lady he thinks is Lady Frances back to his house. However, Saville has replaced the real Lady Frances with a prostitute who is disguised as Lady Frances is. Shamed, Courtall leaves town. The next day, Doricourt, who has been told that Mr. Hardy is on his deathbed, visits him and reluctantly agrees to marry Letitia after all. Then the disguised Letitia enters and reveals her true identity to the overjoyed Doricourt, who also learns that Hardy was not ill after all.

A Bold Stroke for a Husband (1783)
Set in Madrid, the play tells of Don Carlo, who has fled his wife, Victoria, for the courtesan Laura. Laura breaks off with Don Carlo, but she holds on to the documents that entitle her to his land, a gift he foolishly gave her. We learn that Laura is in love with Florio, who is really Victoria disguised as a young man. Meanwhile, Victoria's friend Olivia is resisting efforts by her father, Don Caesar, to marry her off to a series of suitors. In desperation, Don Caesar pretends that he will marry and young girl and then send Olivia off to a convent unless she marries right away. Victoria persuades Olivia's servant to disguise himself as her rich uncle, the original owner of the land that Laura now holds. He convinces Laura that the titles are worthless, so in a rage she rips them up. Victoria reveals herself to Don Carlos, who repents and pledges himself to her again. Meanwhile, Olivia gets married to Julio, the man she wanted all along.